BUILDING AN EXCEPTIONAL HIGH-NET-WORTH PRACTICE

How Accountants Can Become Seriously

Wealthy Working with the Affluent

RUSS ALAN PRINCE

JOHN J. BOWEN JR.

Building an Exceptional High-Net-Worth Practice
How Accountants Can Become Seriously Wealthy Working with the Affluent

By Russ Alan Prince and John J. Bowen Jr.

AES Nation • www.aesnation.com

Printed in China

To Sandi,

Without you, nothing would work right;
everything would fall apart, including me.

Love, Russ

To my wife, Jeanne—it's a privilege
to share my business, life and love with you.

Love, John

Table of Contents

Why You Need This Book 3

A Word About Our Research Methodology. 7

PART I

Becoming Seriously Wealthy: Obstacles and Opportunities. 13

CHAPTER 1   Accountants Under Pressure. 15

CHAPTER 2   Building Significant Wealth 31

PART II

Setting the Foundation for Serious Success. 39

CHAPTER 3   Choose the Optimal Business Model 41

CHAPTER 4   Put Yourself in the Line of Money 51

PART III

Best Practices of Elite Accountants. 65

CHAPTER 5   Build and Manage Your Expert Team 67

CHAPTER 6   Become a Thought Leader 79

CHAPTER 7   Communicate Value Effectively 91

CHAPTER 8   Maximize Wealthy Client Relationships. 107

CHAPTER 9   Generate Referrals from Other Professionals . . . 123

CONCLUSION

Building an Exceptional High-Net-Worth Practice. 139

Why You Need This Book

If you are like most accountants, you are very motivated to become wealthier than you are today—probably a lot wealthier. You may even be among those accountants who are driven to build serious wealth, such as $20 million or more. At the same time, you are committed to providing outstanding service to your clients to help them reach their own financial goals.

We have two clear goals with this book:

- To enable you to build an exceptional high-net-worth practice

- To enable you to profit handsomely by delivering remarkable high-quality services and products in meaningful ways to your wealthy clients

This means sourcing and delivering outstanding value to wealthy, ultra-wealthy and Super Rich clients. (We define the Super Rich as those with a net worth of $500 million or more.) It also means appropriately financially benefiting from delivering high-caliber expertise. Because you will potentially be able to garner commensurate compensation for the outstanding value you deliver, it is possible—with the astute management of your own wealth—for you to become seriously wealthy.

In these pages, we define an elite accountant as one who consistently earns $1 million or more each year. While this is certainly not the norm, we have found it to be a very achievable goal and one that puts you squarely on track to amass meaningful personal wealth.

If your aim is to join the ranks of these elite accountants, this book is for you.

In Part I, we sketch the landscape of the accounting profession today. Accountants are often integral to the financial business achievements and the protection and enhancement of the personal fortunes of the wealthy. The ongoing creation of substantial private wealth translates into substantial opportunities for you to become seriously wealthy yourself—provided you can effectively address the very real obstacles of today's environment.

In Part II, we lay the foundation for your substantial success. Here we encourage you to be thoughtful and deliberate in your selection of your business model and client focus. Having the right business model and the right clients very often means the difference between middling success and an elite practice.

Setting these cornerstones in place will enable you to effectively execute the business development strategies we set out in Part III. These best practices of elite accounting firms can help you reach tremendous professional and financial heights, earning $1 million or more year in and year out. You can potentially become seriously wealthy while doing a remarkable job for your wealthy clients.

If you want to create substantial personal wealth while delivering exceptional value to your wealthy clients, the business development information, insights and methodologies we provide throughout this book will put you on that course. The bottom line is being able to expertly provide your wealthy clients with outstanding value, to communicate that value effectively and to personally achieve greater financial success, which we define as earning $1 million or more—year after year. With these elements in place, you will be poised to become seriously wealthy.

A Word About Our Research Methodology

For a combined total of more than 70 years, we have worked closely with a range of elite professionals whose practices cater to the wealthy. The aim of these professionals is to access the wealthy and provide them with the highest-caliber services and products alongside an incomparable client experience. These elite professionals are not altruists, however. They are highly motivated to make a very good living for themselves, if not to become seriously wealthy.

Complementing our work with elite professionals, we have spent decades studying and consulting to the wealthy, including ultra-wealthy business owners, the Super Rich and single-family offices. The extensive research we have undertaken with these high-net-worth individuals, families and organizations, combined with our in-the-trenches consulting, mentoring and coaching experiences, has translated into an array of technical and behavioral best practices.

In this book, we integrate new empirical and ethnographic research on accountants with our deep knowledge of the wealthy. To ascertain and develop state-of-the-art insights into the best practices of accountants, we conducted a comprehensive survey of senior partners at accounting firms with ten or more partners. We also amalgamated hard-learned lessons from other types of elite professionals such as wealth managers, multifamily offices and private client lawyers.

Our industrywide survey topped off with accounting partners earning $700,000 per year. To capture the perspectives and actions of elite accountants (defined as accounting firm partners earning $1 million or more annually through their high-net-worth practices), we used a chain-referral sampling approach to identify and interview accountants earning a minimum of $1 million a year.

Coupling these two research methods enabled us to discern the differences and similarities among three different income groups: those earning $200,000 to $500,000 a year, those earning $500,000 to $700,000 and those earning $1 million or more each year. Very importantly, it enabled us to precisely identify the best practices of the elite, highest-earning accountants.

In conducting these investigations, we make two important assumptions:

- **All the respondents have integrity.** We assume the accountants surveyed are honest and intent on doing the best job possible for their wealthy clients. (Keep in mind that both saints and sinners would—in responding to a survey or participating in an interview—proclaim they have integrity.)

- **Differences in technical proficiencies—which no doubt exist—are difficult or impossible to ascertain in most surveys.** We therefore presume that all the respondents are technically capable.

Our research tells us that accountants generally run their practices according to one of two business models. We will go into greater detail on each business model later, but for now we'll set out these basic definitions:

- **The product-neutral business model** delivers services in exchange for a retainer, project fees or an hourly fee. The typical services offered via this model are generally administrative, including tax compliance and bill paying, although they sometimes include advanced planning and special projects.

- **The product-inclusive business model** is similar to the product-neutral model but adds in wealth management services and products, which can be provided by an affiliated organization or a third party. In addition to the revenues from fees associated with the product-neutral business model, the product-inclusive business model includes asset-based fees and commissions, depending on the products sold.

As Exhibit A shows, about half of the respondents in our surveys have adopted the product-neutral business model and half use the product-inclusive model.

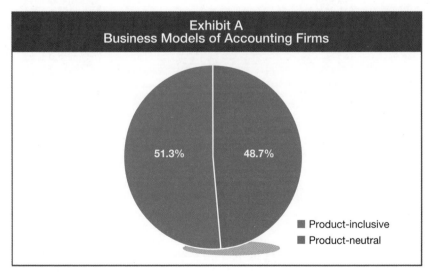

N = 394 partners.
Source: AES Nation.

The best way to determine best practices is to systematically compare respondents based on the incomes they derive from working with the wealthy. We therefore excluded any monies the partners earn from other roles they perform at their accounting firms or because of their partnership interests. We also excluded any incomes they receive from outside business interests.

Exhibit B shows the earning differential between those using the product-neutral business model and those employing the product-inclusive model. As we can see, the incomes of those using the product-inclusive business model tended to generally be higher overall than those of the product-neutral partners.

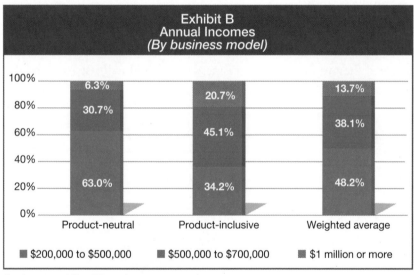

Exhibit B
Annual Incomes
(By business model)

Product-neutral: N = 192 partners.
Product-inclusive: N = 202 partners.
Weighted average: N = 394 partners.
Source: AES Nation.

However—and this is a very important point—the business development best practices of high-net-worth accounting practices that we will present in *Part III: Best Practices of Elite Accountants* are viable for both business models and can result in an income of $1 million or more a year. What matters is choosing the best business model for you and your practice—a topic we'll cover in detail in *Chapter 3: Choose the Optimal Business Model.*

Accountants' choices of business model inform and guide many of their business decisions. Likewise, the incomes they earn reflect to a large degree their effectiveness in implementing best practices for business development. For these reasons, we will highlight where accountants differ and where they are similar, both by business model and by income segment throughout this book.

PART I

Becoming Seriously Wealthy: Obstacles and Opportunities

There are many ways to define professional success. You would probably agree that serving your clients extremely well, building a robust, long-lived practice and creating career opportunities for team members are all important elements of professional success.

And if you are like most accountants, you would agree that building serious wealth is elemental to professional success. In fact, as you will see, about four out of five accountants are very motivated to become meaningfully wealthier than they are today. Our experience tells us that a substantial number of accountants are interested in becoming seriously wealthy, which we define as having financial assets of $20 million or more.

Even as accountants face difficult times due to a dramatically and sometimes adversely changing business environment, the phenomenal and ongoing growth in the creation of private wealth provides enormous opportunities for determined and capable accountants. You have the potential to build an exceptional high-net-worth practice and be well-rewarded for doing so.

CHAPTER 1

Accountants Under Pressure

For the great majority of accountants, earning $1 million annually exclusively from their practices can be a stretch. But as you will see in *Part III: Best Practices of Elite Accountants,* your mastery of key business development strategies can certainly lead to a more substantial and lucrative high-net-worth accounting practice. In this chapter, we will consider the obstacles you probably face to becoming very successful and personally wealthy.

There are numerous industry trends working against the financial success of high-net-worth accountants today. These are four of the more pressing concerns:

- Significantly increasing competition

- The commoditization of expertise (in other words, services and products)

- Fee compression

- Accessing business opportunities with wealthy clients

Looking forward, these are related factors that will—for most accountants—make it harder to excel.

Significantly increasing competition

Overall, nearly nine out of ten accountants in our research reported that competition is significantly increasing. (See Exhibit 1.1.)

Competition is coming from all directions. For example, artificial intelligence is transforming all the professions. Already, robo-advisors are adversely impacting the practices of a growing number of financial advisors, which consequently affects product-inclusive accountants.

As cognitive computing in professional arenas becomes normative, a substantial percentage of product-neutral accountants will find the financial rewards associated with being an accountant increasingly out of their reach. Either smart machines will replace them, or these accountants will play a highly diminished role in the delivery of accounting services.

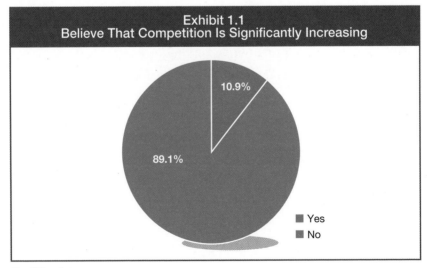

Exhibit 1.1
Believe That Competition Is Significantly Increasing

10.9%

89.1%

■ Yes
■ No

N = 394 partners.
Source: AES Nation.

Relatively speaking, the belief that competition is increasing is somewhat more prevalent among product-neutral accountants. With the perception of greater competition so high, there is little difference among accountants based on income. (See Exhibits 1.2 and 1.3.)

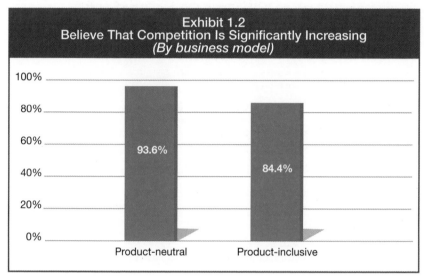

Exhibit 1.2
Believe That Competition Is Significantly Increasing
(By business model)

N = 394 partners.
Source: AES Nation.

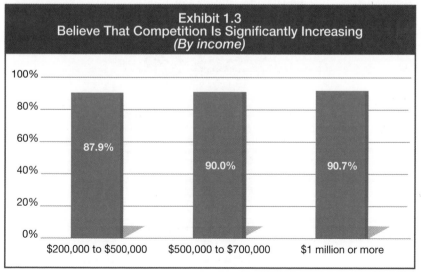

Exhibit 1.3
Believe That Competition Is Significantly Increasing
(By income)

N = 394 partners.
Source: AES Nation.

Increasing competition makes it essential to differentiate your high-net-worth accounting practice. Your ability to deliver Super Rich services and products (see *Chapter 5: Build and Manage Your Expert Team*) and your ability to be a thought leader (see *Chapter 6: Become a Thought Leader*) are instrumental to standing out from the tightly packed crowd.

The commoditization of expertise

As Exhibit 1.4 shows, 85 percent of accountants these days see many of their deliverables as commodities. More than ever before, professionals and their deliverables are fungible.

This does not mean there are not professionals who are more competent and more capable than others; certainly, there are. It is just that there are not any truly unique products and services, and everyone is replaceable. While you might be in the top 10 percent of accountants, we are confident you know other accountants who are also in the top 10 percent.

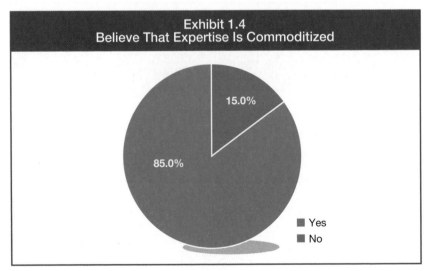

Exhibit 1.4
Believe That Expertise Is Commoditized

15.0%

85.0%

■ Yes
■ No

N = 394 partners.
Source: AES Nation.

Proportionately, somewhat more product-neutral accountants than product-inclusive accountants see greater commoditization of expertise. (See Exhibit 1.5.) This is in line with the attitudes of many in the wealth management industry who believe in the ability to differentiate themselves based on their services and products, as exemplified by investment performance.

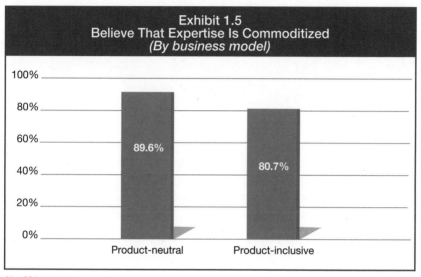

Exhibit 1.5
Believe That Expertise Is Commoditized
(By business model)

N = 394 partners.
Source: AES Nation.

As seen in Exhibit 1.6, the perception of the commoditization of expertise is more prevalent among those earning less. This is likely a function of the issues and needs of their clients. That is, those accountants earning more tend to work with wealthier clients, who often have more-complex situations that require more-sophisticated and therefore less-commoditized solutions.

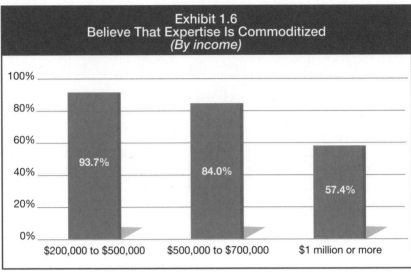

Exhibit 1.6
Believe That Expertise Is Commoditized
(By income)

N = 394 partners.
Source: AES Nation.

The more the offerings of accountants are commoditized, the more easily replaced a particular accountant becomes. To avoid this conundrum, you likely need to work with wealthier clients and be able to offer Super Rich services and products, as we'll discuss in detail in *Chapter 4: Put Yourself in the Line of Money.* At the same time, your ability to access the wealthy on a preferential basis becomes more and more essential.

Fee compression

A pervasive problem for many accountants is fee compression. As Exhibit 1.7 shows, nearly 60 percent of those surveyed feel they are regularly being pressured to lower their fees. This is a product of increasing competition and commoditization.

Fee compression is less of an issue for product-inclusive accountants than for product-neutral accountants. (See Exhibit 1.8.)

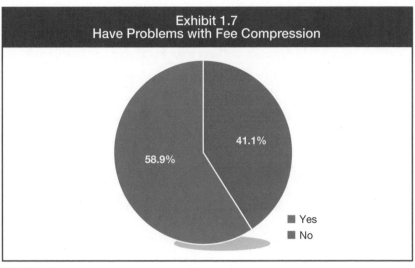

N = 394 partners.
Source: AES Nation.

For the former, many of the fees are "built into" the financial products they offer. Also, many times the fees are paid directly. And in the case of most traditional life insurance policies, the commissions are statutory.

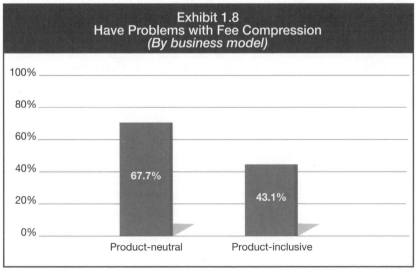

N = 394 partners.
Source: AES Nation.

The more-successful, highest-earning accountants have much less trouble with fee compression, as Exhibit 1.9 demonstrates. We believe a large part of this is because elite accountants are able to explain solutions to clients in highly constructive, effective ways—an issue we'll explore in *Chapter 7: Communicate Value Effectively*. Specifically, when it comes to the fees the most-successful accountants charge, their discussions with wealthy clients and prospective clients are usually about *value* as opposed to *cost*.

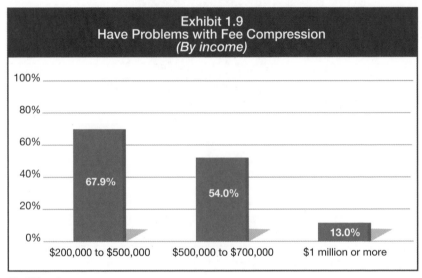

Exhibit 1.9
Have Problems with Fee Compression
(By income)

N = 394 partners.
Source: AES Nation.

Differentiating yourself from your competitors and developing the ability to effectively communicate the value you provide are essential to build a high-net-worth accounting practice and earn $1 million annually. The bottom line? Once you are capable of providing viable solutions to the wealthy, the key to success and consequently your ability to earn $1 million each year is effective business development.

Sourcing business opportunities from the wealthy

There are two considerations when it comes to generating business from the wealthy. One is your ability to maximize your business relationships with your existing affluent clients. The other is your facility at accessing new wealthy clients.

Maximizing business opportunities with current wealthy clients

Overall, nearly three out of five accountants say they are failing to maximize business opportunities with their wealthy clients. This is slightly more the case for product-neutral accountants, compared with product-inclusive accountants. (See Exhibits 1.10 and 1.11.)

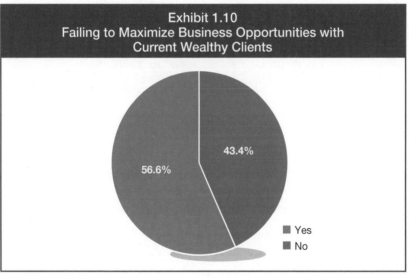

Exhibit 1.10
Failing to Maximize Business Opportunities with Current Wealthy Clients

43.4%

56.6%

■ Yes
■ No

N = 394 partners.
Source: AES Nation.

23

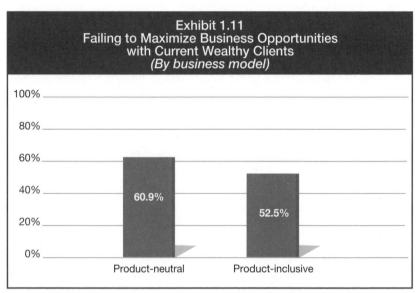

Exhibit 1.11
Failing to Maximize Business Opportunities
with Current Wealthy Clients
(By business model)

N = 394 partners.
Source: AES Nation.

Most telling is that the elite accountants are more likely to maximize business opportunities with their current wealthy clients; only about a quarter of them report that doing so is a problem. (See Exhibit 1.12.) The fact that so many—comparatively speaking—of the most successful accountants are delivering multiple services and products to their wealthy clients is a major contributor to their financial success.

Considering the time, effort and costs required to acquire new wealthy clients, it is only logical for you to maximize these relationships. We regularly find that accountants—and other professionals—are often siloed in their thinking and actions. They focus only on the immediate issues and do not look for additional ways they can deliver value to their wealthy clients. This is a disservice to their affluent clients and to themselves. In *Chapter 8: Maximize Wealthy Client Relationships*, we will delve into this topic and provide you a proven methodology to enable you to identify business opportunities where you can deliver value.

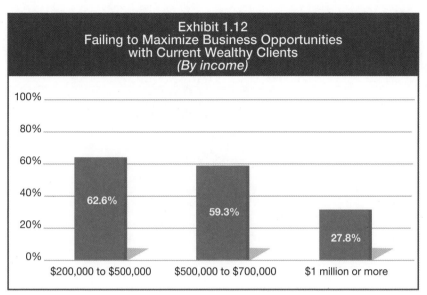

Exhibit 1.12
Failing to Maximize Business Opportunities
with Current Wealthy Clients
(By income)

N = 394 partners.
Source: AES Nation.

Accessing new wealthy clients

Another challenge is being able to access new wealthy clients. Nearly nine out of ten accountants report that it is difficult to source new affluent clients. (See Exhibit 1.13.) Clearly, one of the major objectives and biggest challenges of accountants focused on the wealthy is connecting with them in the first place.

Exhibit 1.14 shows that this perspective is slightly more common among product-neutral accountants, compared with product-inclusive accountants. More informative is that this conundrum is pervasive among accountants earning less than $700,000 annually. It is much less common among elite accountants, with only about half of them considering this to be a major issue. (See Exhibit 1.15.)

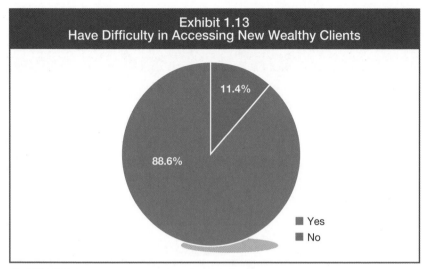

N = 394 partners.
Source: AES Nation.

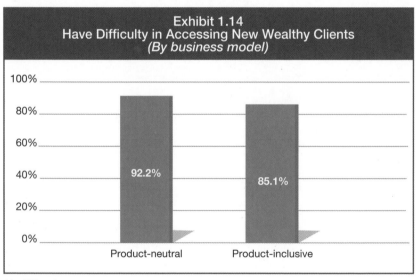

N = 394 partners.
Source: AES Nation.

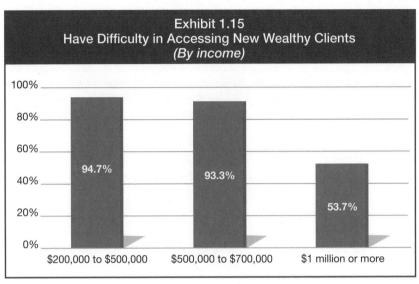

Exhibit 1.15
Have Difficulty in Accessing New Wealthy Clients
(By income)

N = 394 partners.
Source: AES Nation.

Elite accountants—through education as well as trial and error—have tended to identify processes and methodologies that are very effective in sourcing the wealthy. It is these approaches we will be addressing in *Part III: Best Practices of Elite Accountants.*

Excelling will become substantially harder

These pressures translate into the perception that, going forward, it is going to be harder to excel. About 90 percent of the accountants surveyed feel this way, as shown in Exhibit 1.16. In making this determination, the respondents are considering their current financial accomplishments and have concluded that it is only going to get more challenging to achieve or exceed these levels.

Exhibit 1.17 tells us that a meaningfully greater percentage of product-neutral accountants than product-inclusive accountants anticipate a more difficult future. Good investment performance, for example, can enable product-inclusive accountants to do quite well for their affluent clients and their own practices. Scenarios like this do not often exist for product-neutral accountants.

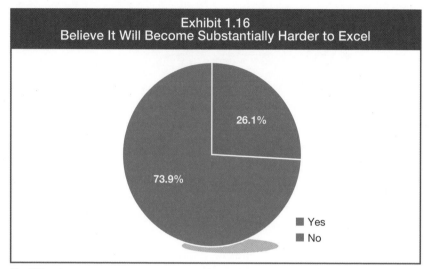

Exhibit 1.16
Believe It Will Become Substantially Harder to Excel

26.1%

73.9%

■ Yes
■ No

N = 394 partners.
Source: AES Nation.

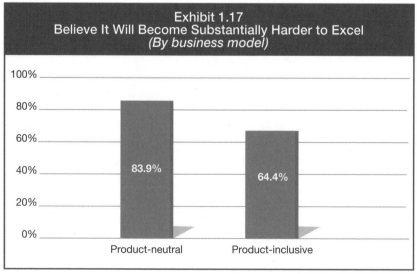

Exhibit 1.17
Believe It Will Become Substantially Harder to Excel
(By business model)

83.9%

64.4%

Product-neutral

Product-inclusive

N = 394 partners.
Source: AES Nation.

Only about 30 percent of the elite accountants are very concerned about achieving at a high level in the future. (See Exhibit 1.18.) Meanwhile, a significantly larger percentage of those earning less are very concerned. The elite accountants—irrespective of business model—are usually implementing business development best practices as well as other best practices that will likely permit them to continue to excel.

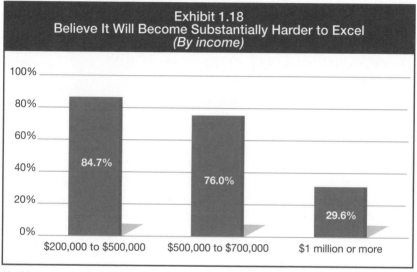

Exhibit 1.18
Believe It Will Become Substantially Harder to Excel
(By income)

N = 394 partners.
Source: AES Nation.

Food for thought

For most accountants, business is only going to get harder. This is the case whether you have a product-neutral or product-inclusive high-net-worth accounting practice. There are a number of structural factors such as greater competition, the commoditization of expertise, and fee compression that are working against you.

Nevertheless, the real issue is this: Do you want to create an accounting practice focusing on the wealthy where you can earn $1 million or more annually?

More effort alone is unlikely to produce more personal income. You need to be able to source high-potential—that is, wealthy—clients. You also need to be able to deliver meaningful value. By adopting the business development best practices of elite accountants as well as the best practices of other professionals working with the wealthy, you can probably build a practice where you earn $1 million or more annually.

CHAPTER 2

Building Significant Wealth

Based on extensive research over decades, we know that for an accountant to consistently earn $1 million or more each year from his or her individual practice is two standard deviations away from the norm. It is the exception, not the rule. However, as we will see, you can very likely apply business development best practices that will enable you to generate the levels of revenue that translate into considerable financial success.

It's also important to note that by applying these business development best practices, you will probably be able to meaningfully raise your income no matter where you are starting from. You might not reach the $1 million level, but you will most likely become substantially more financially successful than you are today.

There are a number of different ways to reach the $1 million or more income level. We are focusing in this book on working with the wealthy— on creating or growing a high-quality high-net-worth practice. In this chapter, we'll explore several different variations of private wealth where accountants can often deliver exceptional value and subsequently derive tremendous personal and financial benefit.

Clients first

We have found that most professionals focusing on the wealthy are highly motivated to do a good job—a quality we consider a necessity. There is no question that there are many professionals who are not as motivated and still make a lot of money. Many times, these professionals, because of a lack of moral fortitude, are willing to stretch or break the rules in search of personal gain, with their clients as the victims.

Putting the needs and wants of your clients first is not only an absolute requirement; it is also good business. Being intensely client-centered is a wonderful foundation for a high-net-worth accounting practice that can earn you $1 million or more year after year, helping you become seriously wealthy.

The desire to become wealthier

The definition of "serious wealth" is subjective, but based on extensive assessments of the wealthy and very broadly speaking, a person is seriously wealthy if he or she has a net worth of $20 million or more. A net worth of $20 million is sometimes called "jet money," as it eliminates the need to fly commercial.

You might have a different definition of serious wealth. However, a more direct question is this: Do you want to be wealthier than you are today? When we put this question to the accountants we surveyed, we found that a little more than four out of five of them do indeed want to be much wealthier. (See Exhibit 2.1.)

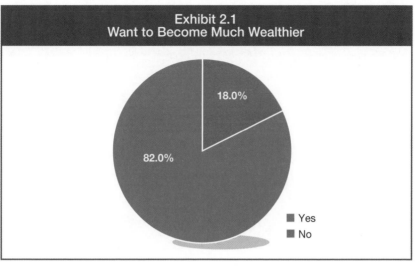

Exhibit 2.1
Want to Become Much Wealthier

18.0%

82.0%

■ Yes
■ No

N = 394 partners.
Source: AES Nation.

Exhibit 2.2 shows that a meaningfully greater proportion of product-inclusive accountants than product-neutral accountants want to become wealthier. The ability to deliver wealth management products tends to result in greater high-net-worth practice revenues and, consequently, potentially greater personal wealth for accountants. Therefore, many product-inclusive accountants see bigger upside and are looking to personally capitalize on that upside.

Interestingly, the greater their annual incomes, the more likely high-net-worth accountants are to strive to become seriously wealthy. (See Exhibit 2.3.) For many professionals, the more money they earn, the more they believe they can continue to earn even more. They regularly see no set ceiling to their ability to create personal wealth.

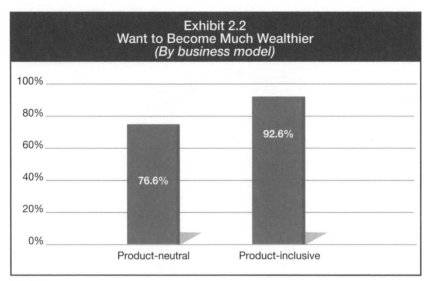

N = 394 partners.
Source: AES Nation.

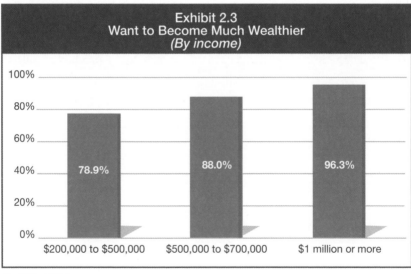

N = 394 partners.
Source: AES Nation.

We have found the same patterns with other professionals such as private client lawyers and wealth managers. Moreover, we see a very strong desire among all successful individuals to excel. Personal wealth creation is one of the results, especially when it comes to successful business owners.

Why successful business owners want to be wealthier

The desire to become seriously wealthy is very common. In an extensive survey of 262 successful business owners (those with financial assets of $1 million or more on top of the equity in their business and other assets, such as a house), almost 95 percent of them want to be wealthier. (See Exhibit 2.4.)

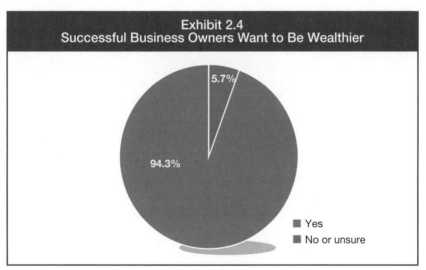

Exhibit 2.4
Successful Business Owners Want to Be Wealthier

N = 262 successful business owners.
Source: Russ Alan Prince and John J. Bowen Jr., *Becoming Seriously Wealthy*, 2017.

People often want to become seriously wealthy for reasons beyond themselves. This was very evident in our study of the 247 successful business owners who want to be wealthier, as Exhibit 2.5 shows.

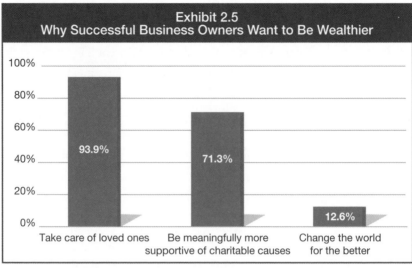

Exhibit 2.5
Why Successful Business Owners Want to Be Wealthier

N = 247 successful business owners.
Source: Russ Alan Prince and John J. Bowen Jr., *Becoming Seriously Wealthy*, 2017.

Greater wealth will not eliminate problems, but it can be very helpful in solving many of them. Most people accept their responsibilities and seek to help those they care about. Moving beyond their own intimate worlds, many people want to be philanthropic. Supporting causes that are dear to them is a viable way to better society, the planet and the lives of others. Some people supercharge this concept and strive to change the world for the better.

As we can see, the great majority of successful business owners strive for greater personal fortunes with the aim of making a more meaningful difference in the lives of people close to them and to charitable causes. A smaller percentage are aiming even higher and thinking globally. This is a far cry from desiring significant wealth because of ego or greed.

When we have empirically delved into this issue, we have consistently found that most business owners, professionals and even a large percentage of the Super Rich are motivated to become wealthier for reasons of caring and concern. In all probability, this is the same with the great majority of accountants, including most likely you.

What it takes to become seriously wealthy

To get on the track to becoming seriously wealthy, you, along with the great majority of accountants, probably need to start with your practice. As it is with the successful and ultra-wealthy business owners and most of the Super Rich (see *Chapter 4: Put Yourself in the Line of Money*), the foundation of personal wealth for most accountants is their profession.

Critical is your ability to deliver exceptional solutions for wealthy clients and ensure that your high-net-worth clients recognize the value you are providing as well as the value you can provide. (See *Chapter 7: Communicate Value Effectively.*)

In addition, high-caliber business development capabilities are essential. You usually will need to be able to maximize wealthy client relationships as well as source new and more-affluent clients. (See *Chapter 8: Maximize Wealthy Client Relationships* and *Chapter 9: Generate Referrals from Other Professionals.*)

By running a high-net-worth accounting practice in this way, you will probably be able to create a substantial financial base. Will this result in serious wealth? Maybe. Will it lead to a meaningful increase in your annual revenue? Almost always—irrespective of whether you use the product-neutral business model or the product-inclusive business model.

While our focus in this book is on helping accountants become more professionally successful sourcing and working with the wealthy, another factor in building significant wealth is often critical. You would be well-advised to maximize your *personal* wealth.

We consistently find that, as is the case with many successful business owners, a substantial proportion of successful accountants are not acting to maximize their personal wealth. To become seriously wealthy, aside from making your practice markedly more successful, you should evaluate your personal financial situation and, if appropriate, take steps to protect and grow your wealth while mitigating taxes. Some of this would certainly entail making use of your own expertise and capabilities. And some of this would require leveraging the abilities of your specialists.

Food for thought

As we saw in the previous chapter, there are a lot of forces working against your becoming professionally successful, let alone earning $1 million or more each year. Still, slightly more than four out of five of the accountants we surveyed want to become much wealthier.

Generally speaking, we have found that professionals and business owners are motivated to become much wealthier so they can better take care of their loved ones and make a difference in their communities and even in the world at large. Critical to your becoming much wealthier is having an astounding high-net-worth accounting practice. We now turn to the foundational elements of an astounding practice: choosing the optimal business model and client focus.

PART II

Setting the Foundation for Serious Success

Having looked at the obstacles and opportunities for today's accountants, we now turn to the underpinnings of serious success in your practice and, subsequently, serious personal wealth.

We want you to be deliberate and thoughtful here. The best starting point is your choice of business model. There is no wrong choice when it comes to your business model, but, as we will see, you must be able to implement business development best practices effectively within your model to realize substantial success.

Second, you should also focus—if at all possible—on a particular segment of the wealthy. For most accountants, irrespective of business model, the segment of choice is successful business owners.

CHAPTER 3

Choose the Optimal Business Model

Your business model is your plan for how you will generate revenue and make a profit. It answers the essential questions: "How do I make money in my practice?" and "What value do I deliver to my clients?"

By way of reminder, here is how we define the two basic business models that accountants generally adopt in serving the wealthy:

- **The product-neutral business model** is built around the delivery of services in exchange for a retainer, project fees or an hourly fee. The typical services offered via a product-neutral business model tend to be administrative. Many accountants using this business model also offer advanced planning for a fee. A number of these accountants also work on custom projects for their clients.

- **The product-inclusive business model** is similar to the product-neutral model but adds in wealth management, including financial products such as investment management and life insurance. Products can be provided by an affiliated organization or a third party, but the relationship and treatment of fees between the accountant and the product issuer must be clear and disclosed upfront. In addition to the fee-for-services revenue associated with the product-neutral business model, the product-inclusive business model allows for asset-based fees and commissions, depending on the products.

If you already serve a wealthy clientele, you most probably employ one of these models. This is a chance to look at your choice with fresh eyes to reconsider whether it continues to be the optimal model for your practice. And if you are looking to move upmarket and begin to serve affluent and ultra-affluent clients, you have an opportunity to choose your ideal business model from the outset.

Income and profitability

As you deliberate your choice of business model, many factors will come to mind. Very likely the first one will be about the potential income and profit each business model can deliver. Here, the question is not just about *how* you will make money, but *how much* money you can make.

Exhibit 3.1 reiterates the earning differential between the two business models. A glance tells us that there are about three times more product-inclusive accountants in the $1 million or more income category than product-neutral accountants. Remember, however, that income is to a great extent a function of effectively implementing business development strategies within your business model; simply choosing the product-inclusive model will not automatically confer a higher income. Also, it is important to note that both business models can enable you to earn $1 million or more per year.

That said, the product-inclusive model does convey a distinct advantage when it comes to profitability. We concluded that in a well-run high-net-worth accounting practice, the margins between the two types of business models differ substantially. Profit margins for the product-neutral practices ranged from 40 to 65 percent, but from 50 to 80 percent for product-inclusive practices. (See Exhibit 3.2.)

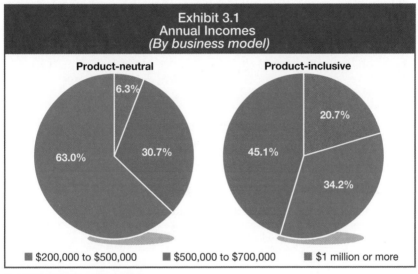

Exhibit 3.1
Annual Incomes
(By business model)

Product-neutral: N = 192 partners.
Product-inclusive: N = 202 partners.
Source: AES Nation.

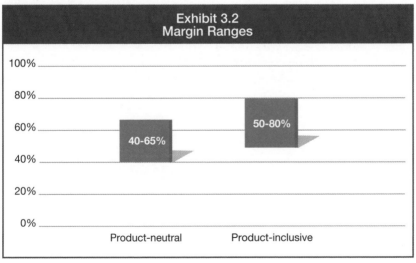

Exhibit 3.2
Margin Ranges

N = 394 partners.
Source: AES Nation.

It's clear that the product-inclusive business model has significantly more potential for profit. This is because the margin is in the products themselves, whereas the revenues of product-neutral accountants predominantly come from time-based fee structures. (However, bear in mind that offering products carries attendant risks and potential for conflict that can arise when assuming fiduciary and similar responsibilities.)

This does not necessarily mean that the product-inclusive business model is right for you. Choosing the product-inclusive model is certainly no guarantee that you will earn a higher income than if you chose the product-neutral business model. Your choice is simply the starting point; how well you execute business development strategies *within* your business model is what will determine your income.

Other factors to consider

In addition to potential for income and profit, there are many other factors to consider when selecting your business model. Take into account your overarching objectives, the operating culture and environment of your accounting firm, your range of in-house capabilities, and the risk-reward differential of each business model.

Exhibit 3.3 compares the key considerations for selecting an accounting practice model.

Exhibit 3.3 Considerations for Selecting a Business Model		
Consideration	Product-neutral	Product-inclusive
Primary objectives	• Revenue growth • Increase opportunities to cross-sell core services • Increase client retention and profitability	• Highest possible profitability from business model and from wealthy clients • Additional sources of revenue
Culture	• Preference for new opportunities that can be implemented with minimal disruption to existing business model • Comfortable with handoffs to outside specialists and experts for certain aspects of client relationships	• Comfortable with innovation and reinvention • Willingness to discuss new products and fee arrangements with existing clients • Ability to shepherd client relationships from inception through and including product sales
Offerings	• Core accounting services • Often other administrative, operational and advanced planning services	• Same as product-neutral offerings, plus financial products and capabilities
Expertise	• Significant in-house expertise • The internal mechanisms to facilitate cross-specialization referrals	• Same as product-neutral expertise, plus willingness to have in-house or to source needed wealth management capabilities from affiliated and third-party providers
Compensation	• Retainer, project and/or hourly fees	• Same as product-neutral, plus asset-based fees, commissions and other incentives such as success fees
External experts	• Most capabilities are in-house or organically developed • Requires limited number of external relationships	• May require a broad range of external relationships to access and deliver a full suite of wealth management solutions

Adopting best practices within each business model

Both the product-neutral and the product-inclusive business models can deliver tremendous upside for high-net-worth accounting practices. Success (and the ability to hit the high end of the margin ranges) is typically contingent on a thoughtful business design and meticulous implementation, which are further supported by best practices for optimizing staffing, infrastructure, internal processes and business development, including new client acquisition efforts.

In the context of the two business models, the implementation of these best practices takes on different tenors. We will go into more detail on best practices in Part III, but for now, consider the interplay between business model and business development best practices. Exhibit 3.4 provides a quick comparison.

Best practice: Have an adaptable infrastructure and operations

The infrastructure an accounting firm needs to support a high-net-worth practice is a function of the nature and range of services it will deliver to the wealthy. The more products and services you offer on the platform, the greater your infrastructure requirements will be.

There are numerous options—including internal, outsourced and hybrid models—that you should carefully evaluate against the human and capital resources of your accounting firm and its overarching goals for your high-net-worth practice.

Closely related to the infrastructure are the operational processes and procedures that employees will follow for seamless implementation and compliant results. It is important to realize that certain affluent client situations may necessitate modifications to existing protocols. These can seem counterintuitive to process-oriented and risk-averse professionals but are a critical part of creating a viable and client-focused high-net-worth practice.

Exhibit 3.4 Best Practices and Business Models		
Best practice	**Product-neutral**	**Product-inclusive**
Have an adaptable infrastructure and operations	Operation that supports administrative, planning and lifestyle services with associated protocols	Enhanced infrastructure and operational requirements due to expanded product capabilities
Employ high-caliber personnel	Proficiency in tax work, administrative services and often planning expertise, with demonstrated ability to handle affluent clientele	Same as product-neutral staffing requirements, plus additional technical aptitudes to support product categories
Build and leverage a powerful personal and professional brand	Communicate expertise across a broad range of issues, emphasizing tax matters	Same as product-neutral, plus demonstrable knowledge of and proficiencies in wealth management
Communicate the value you deliver	A focus on anticipated results customized to the high-net-worth psychology of the client while benefiting from value-based pricing	Same as product-neutral, plus being attentive to the cost structure and benefits of financial products
Source business opportunities from the wealthy	Capable of maximizing affluent client relationships and able to work with a broad range of referral sources and high-net-worth centers of influence	Capable of maximizing affluent client relationships where the number and type of potential referral sources are more restrictive; must have established relationships with productive referral sources that are separate from the accounting practice

Best practice: Employ high-caliber personnel

The wealthy can be, and often are, demanding clients. This means that you must take significant care when selecting and developing your staff. For the long-term success of a high-net-worth accounting practice, you must be able to access and manage high-caliber accountants and other employees who have the requisite skills to work effectively with wealthy clients.

It's often advantageous for an accounting firm to have an ongoing personnel development plan that includes the training, education, mentoring and supervision each team member needs to excel. Without question, lifelong learning is essential for accountants who want to excel in sourcing and working with the wealthy. This is the only way to be constantly and appropriately up to date.

Two areas in particular contribute to the overall effectiveness of a team: technical proficiency and interpersonal behaviors. All staff members should be thoroughly screened for the knowledge and ability needed to oversee everything from individual services (which can range from the mundane, like bill paying, to the highly specialized, such as portfolio construction) to the complete suite of deliverables. This technical expertise should be backed by the demeanor and communications skills that support effective and productive engagement with wealthy clients.

At the same time, critically, you will need to be able to deliver a range of services and products to the wealthy. The capabilities to do this might come from within your accounting firm or in conjunction with external specialists. Your team is essential to business development because it is the foundation of your ability to meet the wants, needs and preferences of affluent clients (see *Chapter 5: Build and Manage Your Expert Team*).

Best practice: Build and leverage a powerful personal and professional brand

The profile of your accounting firm and, more importantly, your professional profile are many times instrumental to the success of your high-net-worth practice. As we will discuss in *Chapter 6: Become a Thought Leader*, being recognized by the wealthy and by other professionals is a very powerful way to establish yourself as an expert. From a business perspective, there are a multitude of benefits to becoming an industry thought leader. Perhaps most important, it is a very potent way to enhance your ability to generate new business.

The complication is that in many accounting firms, accountants have a limited ability to communicate that they indeed have the expertise the wealthy want. You need a concerted process to meaningfully convert insights into opportunities. Furthermore, the wealthy—to a very large degree—do business with people, not firms. Therefore, your branding as a leading authority is what really matters most when it comes to building your high-net-worth practice.

Best practice: Communicate the value you deliver

The capability to deliver value is negated if you fail to communicate that value to the wealthy (see *Chapter 7: Communicate Value Effectively*). All too often, accountants fail to explain in meaningful ways the significance and usefulness of the solutions they are prescribing. It is quite common for accountants to describe the services and products they provide in ways that badly fail to resonate with their wealthy clients.

By adeptly connecting your services and products to what is really important to your affluent clients, you are much more likely to get them to take action. And when you motivate them to act, your high-net-worth accounting practice will thrive.

Best practice: Source business opportunities from the wealthy

One of the most valuable skill sets in the rapidly expanding and increasingly competitive arena for business from wealthy clients is the ability to maximize wealthy client relationships and source new affluent clients.

This requires the ability to truly understand your wealthy clients and to motivate current clients to provide referrals to their peers. Moreover, as is the case with most high-end professional services, the most reliable and productive approach for sourcing new wealthy clients is working with other professionals to facilitate new affluent client referrals.

Food for thought

Working with the wealthy is a high-growth and very profitable practice area for astute accountants. While there are many business model variations accountants can adopt, there are two basic forms: the product-neutral business model and the product-inclusive business model. Neither one is inherently superior; the business model that is most appropriate for you depends on a range of factors.

In *Part III: Best Practices of Elite Accountants*, we will address business development best practices that—with the appropriate tweaking—are applicable to both business models. Whichever business model you choose, it is highly probable that by implementing these best practices, you will be able to meaningfully increase the value you bring to wealthy clients and prospective clients, as well as create greater personal wealth.

An important consideration in building a high-net-worth accounting practice is identifying the type of wealthy clients that have considerable potential—the topic of the next chapter.

CHAPTER 4

Put Yourself in the Line of Money

As we saw in *Chapter 1: Accountants Under Pressure,* there is little doubt that increasingly all services and products are being commoditized, making most professionals—including many accountants—highly fungible. However, by concentrating on sourcing and working with the wealthy, accountants who are truly knowledgeable and adept can effectively differentiate themselves from their competitors.

The wealthy, because of their needs, wants and preferences, demand a high caliber of expertise and servicing—and are willing to pay well for this expertise and service. This means that highly motivated, talented accountants can build substantial high-net-worth practices that earn them $1 million or more each year.

The wealthy can be great clients. To maximize the returns on your work with them, it's smart to concentrate your efforts on those segments of the affluent that produce the greatest returns—what we call being *in the line of money.*

There are several types of wealthy clients that equate—for most accountants—to being in the line of money, including successful business owners, affluent investors and single-family offices. We begin with successful business owners.

Successful business owners

Successful business owners are very often ideal clients for all sorts of professionals. This is because they are the engines of private wealth creation—especially *extreme* private wealth creation. In a study of 376 single-family offices, the senior executives at nine out of ten of them reported that the underlying source of the family's personal fortune was a privately held company. (See Exhibit 4.1.)

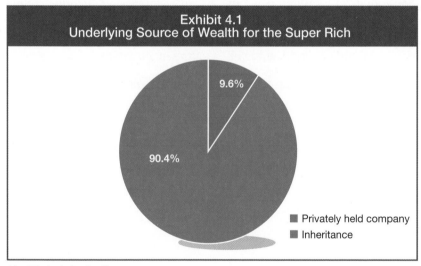

Exhibit 4.1
Underlying Source of Wealth for the Super Rich

9.6%

90.4%

■ Privately held company
■ Inheritance

N = 376 single-family offices.
Source: Russ Alan Prince and John J. Bowen Jr., *Becoming Seriously Wealthy*, 2017.

Not only are successful businesses the primary source of private wealth creation, but they also require and seek out an often-broad array of expertise. Moreover, they will usually pay, and pay well, for high-quality advice. Successful business owners include:

- Owners of family businesses

- Owners of privately held companies

- Owners of professional practices and other types of partnerships

Accountants are regularly the primary "go-to" professionals for successful business owners. In a survey of 513 successful business owners, more than nine out of ten identified their accountants as the professionals they rely on most, as shown in Exhibit 4.2.

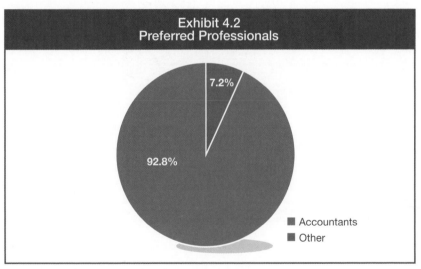

Exhibit 4.2
Preferred Professionals

7.2%

92.8%

■ Accountants
■ Other

N = 513 successful business owners.
Source: AES Nation.

Because so many critical business decisions are entwined with the financials of their companies, these high-caliber entrepreneurs depend on their accountants to help them navigate the possibilities and make wise choices. This is not to say that they do not consult other types of professionals at various times. It is just that they consult accountants more often, and—very importantly—their accountants' erudite opinions carry a great deal of weight.

At the same time, successful business owners are readily identified as ideal clients by about seven out of ten of the accountants surveyed. (See Exhibit 4.3.) They are the top preferred clients of these accountants.

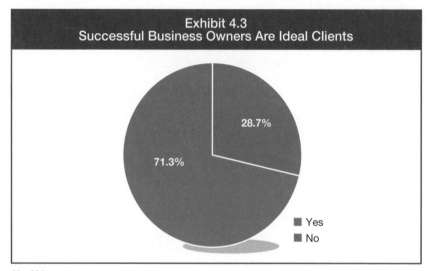

Exhibit 4.3
Successful Business Owners Are Ideal Clients

28.7%

71.3%

■ Yes
■ No

N = 394 partners.
Source: AES Nation.

Meanwhile, nine out of ten product-neutral accountants, compared with about half the product-inclusive accountants, identify successful business owners as ideal clients. (See Exhibit 4.4.) While product-inclusive accountants can deliver the same services as product-neutral accountants, their tendency is to focus to some degree on the products.

When we look at this issue through the lens of income, the relationship between accountants and successful business owners is clear. As Exhibit 4.5 shows, the more money accountants earn, the more likely they are to say that successful business owners are ideal clients.

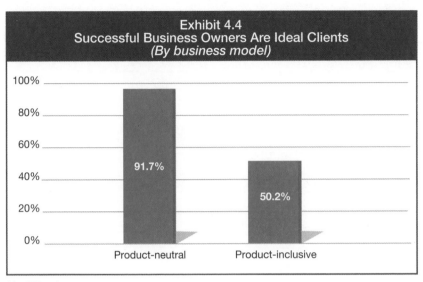

Exhibit 4.4
Successful Business Owners Are Ideal Clients
(By business model)

N = 394 partners.
Source: AES Nation.

Clearly, successful business owners require a significant amount of core accounting and tax work, from compliance to planning. They can also benefit from wealth management on both the personal and the business sides of their lives. By being able to deliver an array of services and products to successful business owners, you can help make them significantly more successful while greatly boosting your own income.

There is no question that there is the potential for great synergistic relationships between successful business owners and their accountants. However, many accountants miss opportunities to create value for their clients and appropriately profit.

For example, in a study of successful business owners, nearly nine out of ten expect to one day sell their companies. At the same time, less than 15 percent have taken any action to mitigate the taxes that would be owed on the sale of their companies. (See Exhibit 4.6.)

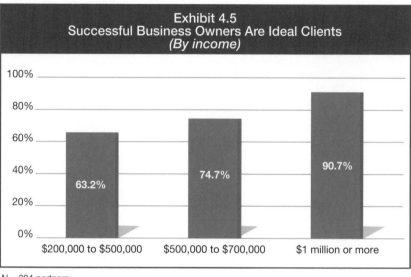

Exhibit 4.5
Successful Business Owners Are Ideal Clients
(By income)

N = 394 partners.
Source: AES Nation.

This creates an excellent scenario for you to provide considerable value to successful business owners. Considering the range of services that business owners planning to sell their companies might need, including formal valuations, restructuring of assets and personal financial planning, it can also be very financially beneficial for you.

Additionally, there is likely to be considerable personal wealth that will require professional management after the sale of a company. Product-neutral accountants will need to refer this business to capable financial advisors. In contrast, product-inclusive accountants will often manage a large percentage—if not all—of the newly liquefied wealth.

There are many scenarios like this one where accountants are perfectly suited to deliver significant value to successful business owners. And as we know through empirical studies that have been soundly confirmed by our in-the-trenches experience, accomplished business owners—when properly approached—are highly inclined to engage their accountants for a diverse and extensive set of expertise.

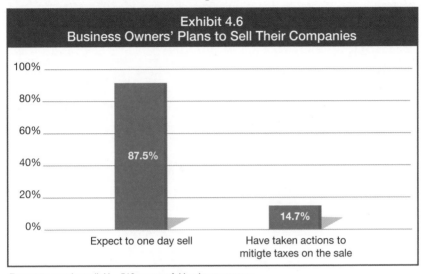

Exhibit 4.6
Business Owners' Plans to Sell Their Companies

Expect to one day sell: N = 513 successful business owners.
Have taken actions to mitigate taxes on the sale: N = 449 successful business owners.
Source: AES Nation.

The major obstacle to accountants securing this business is the inability of most of them to effectively position their services. This is commonly a function of not having a truly in-depth understanding of their clients and prospective clients (see *Chapter 8: Maximize Wealthy Client Relationships*) and of accountants' difficulty connecting their services and products to what is really important to the wealthy (see *Chapter 7: Communicate Value Effectively*).

The financial returns are substantial for accountants who focus on successful business owners and their companies and can systematically identify new opportunities to add value and strategically position their expertise. It is not uncommon for these accountants to literally increase per-client profitability by multiples.

Affluent investors

As Exhibit 4.7 shows, affluent investors are very attractive clients for six out of ten of the surveyed accountants. This is universally the case for product-inclusive accountants, as investment management is a—if not *the*—core deliverable. (See Exhibit 4.8.)

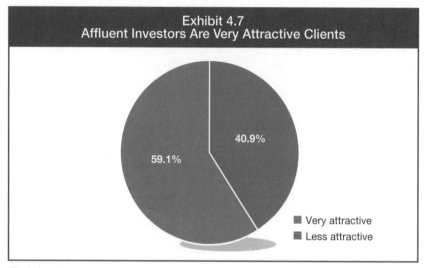

Exhibit 4.7
Affluent Investors Are Very Attractive Clients

40.9%

59.1%

■ Very attractive
■ Less attractive

N = 394 partners.
Source: AES Nation.

However, only about a sixth of the product-neutral accountants see affluent investors as very attractive clients. For these product-neutral accountants, the accounting and tax planning that regularly tie to investment management, including helping evaluate possible solutions, can prove quite rewarding.

The higher their incomes, the more likely accountants are to identify affluent investors as attractive. While five out of six of those earning $1 million or more find affluent investors to be very attractive clients, less than half of those in the $200,000 to $500,000 segment feel the same way. (See Exhibit 4.9.)

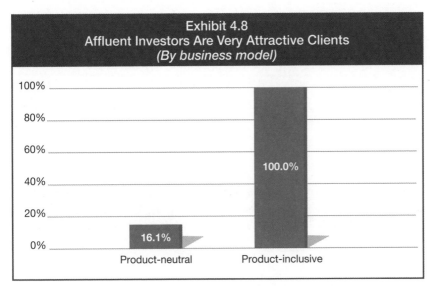

Exhibit 4.8
Affluent Investors Are Very Attractive Clients
(By business model)

N = 394 partners.
Source: AES Nation.

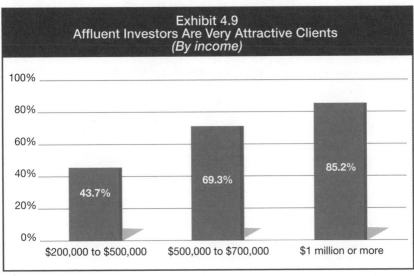

Exhibit 4.9
Affluent Investors Are Very Attractive Clients
(By income)

N = 394 partners.
Source: AES Nation.

As Exhibit 4.10 shows, the "sweet spot" for nearly six out of ten accountants who identify affluent investors as attractive clients are those with between $1 million and $10 million of liquid wealth. A little more than a quarter prefer affluent investors with between $10 million and $25 million of investable assets. One in ten is focused on affluent investors with between $25 million and $50 million in liquid wealth, while the remaining 5.5 percent concentrate on affluent investors with more than $50 million in liquid wealth.

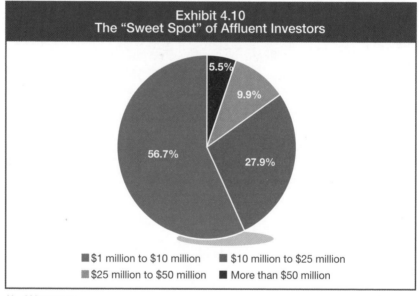

Exhibit 4.10
The "Sweet Spot" of Affluent Investors

- ■ $1 million to $10 million
- ■ $10 million to $25 million
- ■ $25 million to $50 million
- ■ More than $50 million

N = 233 partners.
Source: AES Nation.

Single-family offices

While they are not on the radar screens of many accountants, other types of wealthy clients can provide enormous business opportunities. Specifically, they are the extremely wealthy.

One example is single-family offices. Single-family offices are booming, creating greater demand for the expertise high-net-worth accounting practices can provide. There are a number of sometimes overlapping reasons that single-family offices can be exceptional clients for high-net-worth accounting practices, including these:

- **Opportunities to acquire ultra-affluent clients.** By working with single-family offices, high-net-worth accounting practices create a halo effect that can be leveraged to bring in other ultra-wealthy families as clients. In fact, when ultra-wealthy families become clients because of the reputations of accounting practices as thought leaders working with single-family offices, the ultra-wealthy turn out to be, in the aggregate, more profitable for these practices than the very profitable single-family office clients.

- **Opportunities to become an outsource partner.** As single-family offices become higher-functioning, their senior management and the ultra-wealthy families they serve are increasingly inclined to strategically outsource. They tend to focus on a small set of deliverables and turn to outstanding external experts for other services and products. In effect, a meaningful number of them are disaggregating. This provides tremendous opportunities for high-net-worth accounting practices to acquire tax and compliance work.

- **Investment management opportunities.** Single-family offices make extensive use of investment professionals. Product-inclusive accounting practices can, in the right circumstances, provide investment management expertise to these financial and lifestyle boutiques.

- **Opportunities with international clients.** International single-family offices are often looking for other firms to provide services and

61

support to family members traveling to other countries as well as to provide on-the-ground oversight of investments in those countries. The most likely professionals to provide outpost family office services are high-net-worth accounting practices.

- **Diverse range of additional opportunities.** Single-family offices tend to have a multitude of needs and wants. Consequently, high-net-worth accounting practices can be positioned to address an array of issues and matters from technology requirements to valuation of business interests to managing the plethora of special projects these offices often have.

- **Compensation.** When the fees charged by high-net-worth accounting practices are properly positioned to single-family offices, they are not a problem. That is, by focusing on and communicating value and highlighting differentiated (as opposed to commoditized) offerings, high-net-worth accounting practices can be well-compensated for their services.

In sum, the exceptionally wealthy in general and single-family offices in particular are regularly extremely lucrative clients for talented, capable and forward-thinking accountants. Single-family offices have various needs and wants and are quite willing to pay—and pay well—for high-quality solutions and very fast responsiveness.

We recognize that the exceptionally wealthy are not particularly good clients for many accountants. Still, if you employ the methodologies for obtaining wealthy client referrals from other professionals (see *Chapter 9: Generate Referrals from Other Professionals*), there is a strong possibility that you will end up with some Super Rich clients.

Food for thought

Successful business owners are the preferred clients for many high-net-worth accounting practices—especially the more accomplished ones. These business owners have a diverse and extensive set of needs, wants and preferences, potentially providing tremendous opportunities for you to add value and thus benefit economically.

Affluent investors are extremely and universally attractive to product-inclusive accountants for obvious reasons. Meanwhile, only about 16 percent of product-neutral accountants are interested in affluent investors. There are also other types of wealthy clients that can prove very profitable for accountants. One example is single-family offices.

Keep in mind that if you become a recognized expert with respect to a particular client segment, you dramatically increase your ability to generate revenue that can translate into money in your pocket. To this end, thought leadership can play a powerful role (see *Chapter 6: Become a Thought Leader*).

█████ ████████ ████

PART III

Best Practices of Elite Accountants

New business from the wealthy is essential to almost all accountants who want to earn annual incomes of $1 million or more. While there are other significant factors that contribute to this level of success, we will delve into what is often the most difficult challenge of a great many accountants serving the wealthy: effective business development.

We have found that the most-elite accountants are adept at business development—at least compared with their less financially successful peers. Elite accountants can deliver a broad range of solutions, which is dependent on being able to build and manage a high-caliber team. They are appropriately recognized for their expertise. They do a good job of explaining their services and products. They are able to provide multiple solutions to their wealthy clients. And, very importantly, they are able to motivate other professionals to refer affluent individuals and families to them.

In our experience, these elite accountants are not doing anything you probably cannot also do. It is usually a matter of knowing what to do and then acting. Here in Part III, we will explain what to do and how to do it.

CHAPTER 5

Build and Manage Your Expert Team

In serving the wealthy, there are no polymaths. One individual cannot possibly have the knowledge, skills and wherewithal to deliver the diverse array of solutions the wealthy need and want. Consequently, you need a team—a great one.

Your ability to surround yourself with high-caliber professionals and astute, capable staff will often be essential for building a high-net-worth accounting practice that enables you to earn $1 million or more annually. It's important to realize that not only must you identify the specialists you need, but you must manage the interrelationships between your experts and your affluent clients. Skillfully managing these relationships is often the more complicated part of the two.

As we will see, the nature of the relationships between you and your team of experts differs depending on whether you have adopted the product-neutral business model or the product-inclusive business model. Nevertheless, in both cases, it's very important to always recognize that your clients are *your* clients and not those of your experts. Bottom line: If anything goes wrong or anyone fails to deliver, it is your responsibility. Therefore, your obligation is to ensure you have the appropriate experts as part of your team and that they all know how to "play nice together in the sandbox."

The problems with team members

To be clear, by *team members* we mean other professionals—specialists— that you bring into wealthy client situations to augment your capabilities and deliverables. Remember: These are your experts. You chose them. They are not professionals unassociated with you that your wealthy clients are engaging. Team members can be internal to your accounting firm or they can be external professionals with whom you have formal or informal strategic relationships.

While such experts are often needed, the complication is that about three out of five accountants have experienced severe problems with team members, as Exhibit 5.1 shows.

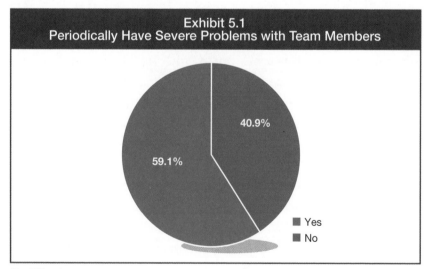

N = 394 partners.
Source: AES Nation.

These problems are more prevalent among product-inclusive accountants than among product-neutral accountants. (See Exhibit 5.2.) Most likely this is a function of product-inclusive accountants having more team members, and ones who often have very strong agendas.

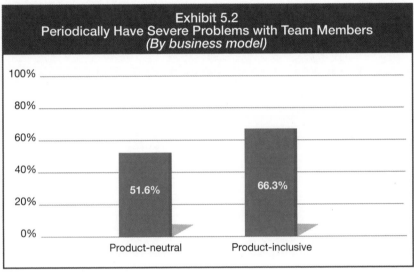

Exhibit 5.2
Periodically Have Severe Problems with Team Members
(By business model)

N = 394 partners.
Source: AES Nation.

Relatively speaking, very few elite accountants are plagued by problems with their team members, as shown in Exhibit 5.3. Clearly, these high-earning accountants are managing the process of everyone working together quite effectively. They are often more systematic in building and managing their teams, using a process we will describe later in this chapter.

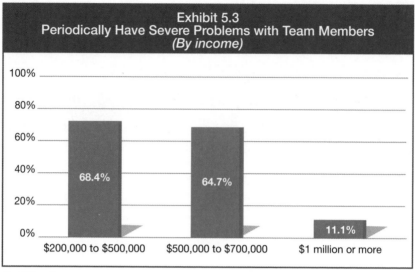

Exhibit 5.3
Periodically Have Severe Problems with Team Members
(By income)

N = 394 partners.
Source: AES Nation.

Problems with team members can prove to be highly detrimental to high-net-worth accounting practices. More than eight out of ten surveyed accountants who report having serious problems with team members say they have lost wealthy clients because of team members. (See Exhibit 5.4.)

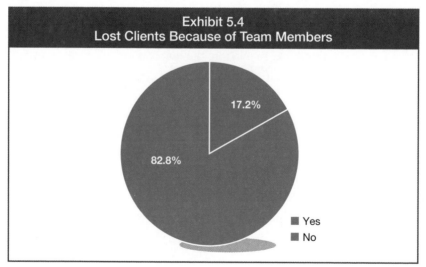

Exhibit 5.4
Lost Clients Because of Team Members

N = 394 partners.
Source: AES Nation.

The loss of wealthy clients due to issues with team members is more prevalent among product-inclusive accountants than among product-neutral accountants, as seen in Exhibit 5.5.

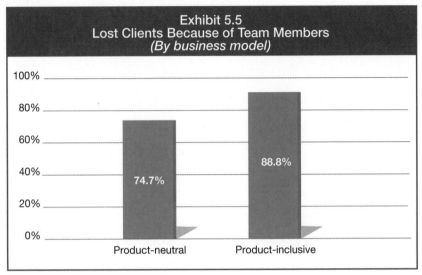

Exhibit 5.5
Lost Clients Because of Team Members
(By business model)

N = 233 partners.
Source: AES Nation.

Exhibit 5.6 illustrates key problems with team members. The most severe problem most accountants confront is specialists pushing their own services and products. This is very characteristic of specialists who have a hammer and see most client situations as a nail. This lack of alignment can translate into major complications and even legal conflicts. What you need to do—from the very beginning—is make absolutely certain everyone is on the same page. The needs, wants and preferences of your wealthy clients should always come first.

About three-quarters of the product-inclusive accountants with team member issues identify compensation disagreements as a severe problem. This is a function of sharing revenues, which in turn is predicated on the value each party brings to a scenario. Meanwhile, less than one in five of

71

the product-neutral accountants reporting team problems see this as a major concern. When it is, the issue is that the specialist is charging too much.

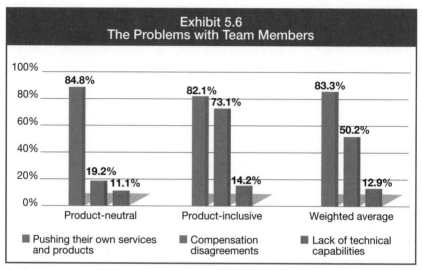

Exhibit 5.6
The Problems with Team Members

Pushing their own services and products • Compensation disagreements • Lack of technical capabilities

Product-neutral: N = 99 partners.
Product-inclusive: N = 134 partners.
Weighted average: N = 233 partners.
Source: AES Nation.

Less than a sixth of the accountants overall point to a lack of technical capabilities as a severe problem. When accountants think specialists they are relying on are not technically proficient, they will regularly drop them in favor of other—more adept—specialists.

Clearly, it's quite important to have a well-run team. If you want to excel in sourcing and working with the wealthy, it's often essential that you and your expert team be able to deliver Super Rich services and products.

Products and services for the Super Rich

Thanks in part to dramatic advances in technology (such as the applications of artificial intelligence, the exponential growth of calculating power, and the ability of leading experts to take one-off solutions and commoditize them), it has become increasingly common for the services and products being used by the family offices, the Super Rich and ultra-wealthy business owners to be made available to a much broader audience.

It's important to bear in mind that your clients do not have to be Super Rich themselves to benefit from these services and products. These solutions can be used by a substantial number of affluent individuals and families to significantly increase or protect their personal wealth.

We define Super Rich services and products as wealth management services and products, as well as legal strategies, that meet three criteria:

1. The ultra-wealthy, the Super Rich or family offices frequently implement them.

2. Many of the wealthy, such as successful business owners and affluent investors, can use them to help themselves become seriously wealthy.

3. High-caliber professionals, such as very capable accountants and their teams, are needed to implement them.

Your ability to provide expert perspectives on a product or service (if you have a product-neutral accounting practice) or to deliver the product or service (if you have a product-inclusive accounting practice) can significantly differentiate you from your competitors. Consequently, you would be well-served if you or someone on your team had expert knowledge of various products and services for the Super Rich, along with experience in implementing them.

Building and managing your team

Most accountants evolve their teams based on the expanding demands and preferences of their wealthy clients. This tends to leave holes that they fill with a just-in-time approach. You probably have a team with gaps that you would quickly seek to close if one of your wealthy clients needed a solution you presently are unable to provide.

We recommend a four-step methodology for building and managing a top-flight team of specialists, starting from scratch. In helping accountants structure state-of-the-art teams, we have found that approaching the issue in this systematic way enables them to upgrade the expertise they can deliver as well as effectively fill in the gaps.

Step 1: Understand your core competencies

In extensively researching the best practices of various types of professionals who focus on the wealthy, we see that understanding one's foundational competencies is a very dominant trend. It is a trend that's also very characteristic of the most accomplished entrepreneurs, including a great many of the Super Rich. We call this trend being "centered."

The very best concentrate their efforts on what they do quite well—their core competencies—and are comfortable with and capable of delegating other functions and responsibilities to the top-quality professionals and staff they oversee. You need to become very clear about just what your core competencies truly are and concentrate on them. To do this, you first must delineate your core professional competencies.

To identify these competencies, answer three questions:

1. What are you extremely good at that is instrumental to the success of your high-net-worth accounting practice?

2. What are you good at that is *not* essential for you to do for your high-net-worth accounting practice to make it very successful?

3. What are you *not* particularly good at that *is* essential for you to do for your high-net-worth accounting practice to make it very successful?

Focus your time and efforts on your answer to the first question. The answers to the other two questions should—in most cases—be delegated to staff and specialists. We have found that too many professionals get wrapped up in doing what is uncovered by the second question. And many professionals feel they are so valuable that they end up spending enormous time and resources dealing with functions unearthed in the third question.

Step 2: Determine specialists with whom to work on client situations

There will be many times when you will need to bring in top-of-the-line specialists to help address the needs, wants and preferences of wealthy clients. These are areas where you are delivering value to the wealthy, but they are not your particular area of expertise—not your core competencies. The specialists you bring to the table are there to supplement and support the services and products you provide the affluent. These experts can come from within your accounting firm or can be specialists you turn to who work at other firms.

There are three criteria to consider when deciding on particular specialists:

*   **Integrity.** You need to deal only with professionals who are scrupulously honest.

*   **Competence.** You want specialists on your team who are both technically and interpersonally extremely capable.

- **Experience.** You need the specialists to not be novices when it comes to the types of wealthy clients you are bringing to the table.

Central to deciding on particular specialists is whether everyone is able to work well together. This requires specifying, in advance, your working arrangements.

Step 3: Establish the ground rules, including all financial arrangements

You will be well-served if you can extensively delineate how you and your specialists will work with your wealthy clients. These are some of the questions you will need to answer:

- Who takes the lead with each wealthy client and precisely what does this mean?

- How will the various products and services be communicated to each affluent client?

- Who makes the final decisions as to what to present to each affluent client?

- When are you brought into the discussions between each of your specialists and your wealthy clients?

- How are conflicts resolved when "wires get crossed"?

By being very clear from the beginning about the working arrangements among all your experts, you are likely to avoid all sorts of problems down the line.

At the same time, the financial arrangements between you and your specialists must be clearly stipulated and will often need to be shared with wealthy clients. This goes for both the product-neutral business model and the product-inclusive business model. For example, if you are a product-neutral accountant and you refer your affluent investor clients to a wealth manager, any sharing of revenue must be disclosed. (And at that point, should you begin sharing revenue, you would be considered a product-inclusive accountant.)

When it comes to setting the ground rules, being tyrannical is rarely productive. On the other hand, you do need to always be in charge. These are your affluent clients, and you are ultimately responsible for the services and products they receive, as well as for the quality of their experience with you and the specialists you are using.

Step 4: Refine your process

While we are talking about this process as if it were linear, the reality is that you will likely need to make modifications. You need an ongoing iterative approach that you can adjust as needed.

As the dynamics of the industry change and as the requirements and desires of the wealthy change, the way you manage and operate your team will have to adjust accordingly. You are responsible for making sure the necessary refinements are made and verified.

Food for thought

Because of the often-complex situations of wealthy clients, you will very likely need to put together and manage a team of high-caliber specialists. What is very telling is that working with these experts has sometimes proven counterproductive for accountants, resulting in them losing wealthy clients.

By setting the ground rules and getting buy-in from all your experts, you will regularly be able to ensure that your wealthy clients are being best-served and that your team is running smoothly with you in charge. Keep in mind that you will need to evaluate your team on an ongoing basis and likely make some refinements to your ground rules and team composition as circumstances change.

Being able to shine in a competitive environment is characteristic of many elite accountants. They are thought leaders, and as we will see in the next chapter, you too can be a thought leader.

CHAPTER 6

Become a Thought Leader

Thought leadership is a very viable and, many times, almost essential component to creating an exceptional high-net-worth accounting practice that enables you to earn at least $1 million per year. There are extensive business benefits to being a thought leader, including the ability to source and retain wealthy clients over extended time periods and to generate new engagements from them.

Being a thought leader can also be a very powerful way to facilitate obtaining wealthy client referrals. You can even employ intellectual capital as a means of "compensating" other professionals for providing affluent client referrals to you.

What is a thought leader?

Some people take a very expansive view of the term, wrapping internal strategy and corporate culture into their definition. Other pundits are more constrained in their definition. As a result, there are many definitions of the term "thought leader."

The way we conceptualize and define thought leadership highlights and emphasizes the potentially exponential business-oriented rewards of being a thought leader. Hence, no one can be a thought leader unless he or she is capitalizing on the dramatically enhanced brand equity attained by the stature conveyed by being a thought leader.

Based on decades of working with elite professionals, their firms and other types of organizations, we have a two-part definition of what constitutes a thought leader.

The first part of our definition is about how others perceive a thought leader:

A thought leader is an individual or firm that is recognized by clients, prospective clients, referral sources, intermediaries and even competitors as one of the foremost authorities in selected areas of specialization. As a result, the individual or firm is their go-to expert.

Brilliance is a function of acclaim, created where others bestow the accolades. Consequently, others anoint accountants as thought leaders.

We now move to the second part of the definition, which is about the commercial component of thought leadership:

A thought leader is an individual or firm that significantly profits from being recognized as the go-to expert.

To become a thought leader, it is especially critical that you monetize the expertise you share. You accomplish this by dramatically increasing your ability to source and to more quickly close wealthy prospective clients, as well as your ability to generate meaningful new opportunities with existing wealthy clients.

The importance of being a thought leader

Being a thought leader is a form of reputational capital. A number of factors are often critical when wealthy prospective clients decide which high-net-worth accounting practice to patronize. Many factors favor thought leaders, including these:

- The more complicated and involved the offerings, the more the wealthy are disposed to turn to recognized state-of-the-art accountants—thought leaders.

- The more difficult it is for wealthy clients to directly evaluate and compare services and products—and it is usually difficult—the more appealing thought leaders become.

- The more detrimental and potentially adverse the consequences of choosing the wrong accountant can be, the more effort the wealthy will make to find what they would define as the best—and the best are often thought leaders.

Because of the potential for damage to their own reputations, many other professionals are often fairly reticent about making referrals to accountants. This might very well even be the case with other accountants at your firm. Thought leadership makes it increasingly easy for other professionals to refer their high-net-worth clients to you for these reasons:

- **Thought leadership validates your expertise.** The fact that these professionals can point to your stature and standing as a thought leader enables them to comfortably and actively recommend you to their wealthy clients with greater confidence and legitimacy.

- **It allows referrers to more easily communicate your expertise.** When making introductions, it is not uncommon for professionals to not be very practiced at making the case for you. Enabling the referral source to use and leverage your thought leadership content can be very useful in eliminating this problem.

- **It acts as currency for qualified introductions from other professionals.** Thought leadership content that helps other professionals to become more successful is a very powerful form of currency. It motivates them to proactively identify and introduce their wealthy clients to you because you are providing information and insights.

About nine out of ten of the surveyed accountants recognize the value of being a thought leader in order to enhance business development activities, as Exhibit 6.1 shows. With all the industry attention being paid to the concept of thought leadership, this finding is not surprising.

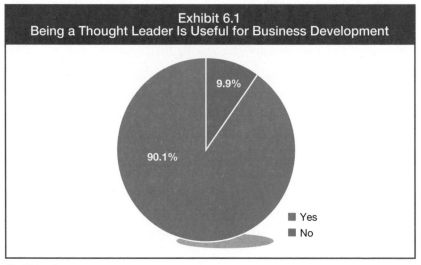

Exhibit 6.1
Being a Thought Leader Is Useful for Business Development

9.9%

90.1%

■ Yes
■ No

N = 394 partners.
Source: AES Nation.

While almost all say that becoming a thought leader is good for business, only about two out of five are actively working to become thought leaders. There is no appreciable difference between the two business models on this issue. (See Exhibits 6.2 and 6.3.)

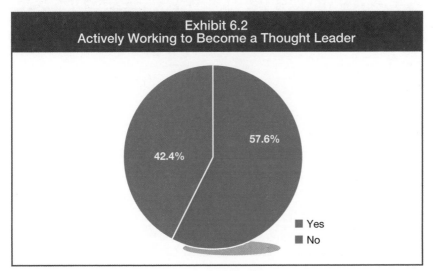

Exhibit 6.2
Actively Working to Become a Thought Leader

57.6%

42.4%

■ Yes
■ No

N = 394 partners.
Source: AES Nation.

Exhibit 6.3
Actively Working to Become a Thought Leader
(By business model)

100%

80%

60%

40%

43.2%   41.6%

20%

0%

Product-neutral   Product-inclusive

N = 233 partners.
Source: AES Nation.

What is most insightful is that, as shown in Exhibit 6.4, the great majority—nearly all, in fact—of the most financially successful accountants are striving to become thought leaders.

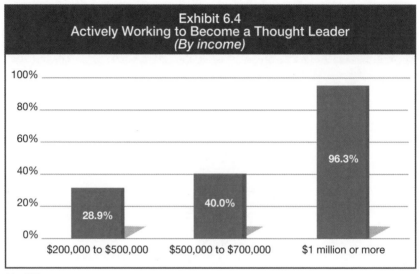

Exhibit 6.4
Actively Working to Become a Thought Leader
(By income)

N = 394 partners.
Source: AES Nation.

In surveys of professionals focusing on the wealthy, we commonly find that the more economically accomplished professionals are taking concerted steps to become and continue to be seen as thought leaders. They are able to do this in part because their greater success gives them the financial resources to commit to the endeavor. However, today there are very powerful ways you can become a thought leader with minimal cost. For the great majority of accountants, the answer is curating content, which we will discuss next.

How to become a thought leader

There are four major steps to becoming a thought leader:

1. Determine your approach to becoming a thought leader.

2. Develop a steady stream of thought leadership content.

3. Deliver your thought leadership content.

4. Follow up to monetize your thought leadership content.

Step 1: Determine your approach to becoming a thought leader

If you want to proactively become a thought leader, there are two questions you need to answer:

- **What audiences do you want to think of you as a leading authority?** To become a thought leader, you will have to prove to certain audiences that you are an expert. Therefore, usually a good way to start the process of becoming a thought leader is to have a solid understanding of the audiences you are focusing on. For nearly all accountants, there are likely to be multiple audiences.

- **What do you want your audiences to identify as your areas of expertise?** This is why clients, prospective clients and other professionals should consult with you. There are different perspectives on being a thought leader, from being the authority with respect to a specific product such as investment management to being the go-to source for information on dealing with a broad range of high-net-worth issues and concerns. (The latter is one of the most effective types of positioning.)

Over time you will likely need to modify your approach. You might even change direction to adjust to altering circumstances. While the process is a constant, your "expertise" will likely need to adapt to a changeable environment.

Step 2: Develop a steady stream of thought leadership content

Critical to becoming a thought leader and maintaining this professional stature is developing a steady stream of information and insights. Consistency is a necessity.

A good way to think about becoming a thought leader is to view it as a campaign. You will most likely need to be able to provide a steady stream of thought leadership content on an ongoing basis in order for your audience to see you as a definitive expert. This means you need a great deal of thought leadership content. There are two nonexclusive approaches you can take to providing a steady stream of thought leadership content.

Approach #1: Create thought leadership content. When you create thought leadership content, you are building new ideas, concepts or solutions for particular audiences. A common way for high-net-worth accounting practices to create intellectual capital is to leverage their experts in a particular area such as investing, planning or taxes.

While creating thought leadership content can be a very powerful approach, it has drawbacks, including these:

- Regularly creating thought leadership content requires its own set of specialized expertise, such as proficiency in survey methodologies.

- In many environments, creating thought leadership content has limited long-term potential considering the need to supply on ongoing stream of thought leadership content.

- Creating and replenishing a steady supply of thought leadership content is often a costly endeavor.

Because of the difficulties in creating thought leadership content, for the great majority of accountants, the second approach—curating thought leadership content—is the optimal one.

Approach #2: Curate thought leadership content. The ability to pull together ideas, concepts, strategies, products and so forth that are meaningful and of strong interest to particular audiences is an extraordinarily effective way for you to provide a steady stream of high-caliber thought leadership content.

It is evident that curating thought leadership content is an exceptionally effective methodology and is a comparatively inexpensive way to become a leading authority. It's especially useful because curating enables you to deliver thought leadership content on an ongoing basis, and you can become more highly knowledgeable about state-of-the-art services products, types of clients, best practices of various types of professionals and so forth. In addition, curating content is, for most accountants, a very inexpensive way to provide thought leadership content that has "heuristic punch"—that is, it is easy for the intended audiences to understand and potent enough to set the stage for action.

Having the intellectual capital is necessary, but that alone is insufficient to become a thought leader. You still have to deliver it to your intended audiences.

Step 3: Deliver your thought leadership content.

With thought leadership content in hand, you now can use it to position yourself as the leading authority. This means connecting with your audiences: prospective clients, current clients and other professionals. There are a number of ways to deliver your intellectual content:

- **Packaged content.** This is making your thought leadership content tangible in different formats, such as reprinted articles, reports and books. This is an amazingly powerful way to communicate that you are a thought leader.

- **Social media.** Podcasts, blogs and wikis are proving to be an increasingly effective way to distribute thought leadership content.

- **Live events.** From the perspective of business development, it is often critical to "press the flesh." However, a solid intermediary step and a very potent way to communicate your thought leadership content is to participate in events.

For many accountants, live events, from speaking at a conference to speaking at a breakfast meeting, are the best way to deliver thought leadership content. Live events also easily lend themselves to directly connecting with the people you want to reach.

Step 4: Follow up to monetize your thought leadership content

Without well-orchestrated follow-up, you have a diminished possibility of making money. That is not to say that thought leadership initiatives will not stalwartly buff your professional brand, which in turn helps cultivate new wealthy clients as well as more business from existing affluent clients. It is also not to say that thought leadership initiatives will not bring in new business over the transom. There is plenty of proof that both these scenarios will indeed occur. However, while getting new business these ways is a good thing, if you really want to sincerely and dramatically benefit from being a thought leader, you need to reach out actively to wealthy clients, prospective clients and other professionals.

Critical to follow-up is getting the in-person meeting. Being a thought leader is very much about making it both easier and much more probable that you will get those meetings on a very preferential basis.

Food for thought

Being a thought leader is likely to become a major differentiator among accountants, irrespective of the business model they adopt. Your ability to stand out from the multitude of other professionals seeking to do business with the affluent will be essential if you want to earn $1 million or more annually.

Indispensable to becoming a thought leader is providing a steady stream of high-caliber content to wealthy clients, affluent prospective clients and other professionals. For most accountants, the optimal approach is to curate thought leadership content. It is also very important to be able to skillfully deliver the content. For many professionals—including accountants—this often takes the forms of sending out packaged content and making presentations at live events.

CHAPTER 7

Communicate Value Effectively

The better accountants—whether product-neutral or product-inclusive—are intent on delivering the best solutions for their wealthy clients. It's a matter of integrity.

A complication faced by many accountants as well as other professionals is needing to effectively explain what they are advising and why they should be well-compensated for their expertise. As we noted in *Chapter 1: Accountants Under Pressure*, 85 percent of accountants surveyed believe their services and products are becoming increasingly commoditized, and about three out of five say they are facing fee compression.

By smartly communicating your value, you not only mitigate these problems, but you also help your wealthy clients make better use of your expertise. Specifically, they will be much more inclined to follow your recommendations. There are a number of considerable benefits you incur when you are adept at communicating value:

- **You increase the continuity of your relationships with wealthy clients.** The affluent are less likely to switch accountants when they understand the value they are receiving. For product-inclusive accountants, an added advantage is that if investment performance stumbles, for instance, the affluent investor is more inclined to stay with you, giving you the opportunity to get his or her investment performance back on track.

- **You have more and stronger opportunities to maximize client relationships.** By communicating your value well, you become better and better positioned to provide a wide array of expertise to your wealthy clients—something we discuss more in the next chapter.

- **You increase the likelihood of receiving client referrals.** Wealthy clients who see real value in what you provide because you make the effort to tie what you are delivering to what is important to them will more readily and more enthusiastically refer you to peers and loved ones.

It's evident from our research with accountants, as well as our research with other professionals, that there is often a lot of room for improvement when it comes to effectively communicating value.

Accountants see room for improvement

By definition:

Communicating value is a function of connecting the services and products you provide with the agendas of particular wealthy clients.

We have found that a little more than two-thirds of the accountants surveyed believe they need to do a better job of connecting their services and products to client benefits. (See Exhibit 7.1.) They usually reach this conclusion for several reasons:

- They are too often failing to close business in scenarios where the value they will provide is appreciably greater than the cost.

- They are getting considerable pushback from wealthy clients because these clients have different and often unrealistic expectations of specific services and products.

- They find their wealthy clients are expressing discontent to other professionals and potential clients.

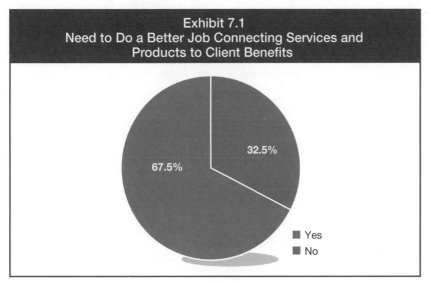

Exhibit 7.1
Need to Do a Better Job Connecting Services and
Products to Client Benefits

N = 394 partners.
Source: AES Nation.

As Exhibit 7.2 shows, a meaningfully higher percentage of product-neutral accountants than product-inclusive accountants believe they need to do a better job of communicating value. This distinction is in part a function of the perceived commoditization of expertise, which is more prevalent among the product-neutral accountants.

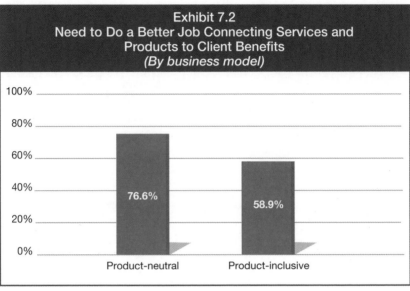

N = 394 partners.
Source: AES Nation.

It is also informative that this perspective is more pervasive among accountants earning less, as seen in Exhibit 7.3. While just one in five of the accountants earning $1 million or more annually believes they need to be more effective in connecting services and products to client benefits, two-thirds of the accountants earning between $500,000 and $700,000 and four out of five accountants earning between $200,000 and $500,000 see this as an issue. The ability of elite accountants to communicate value—to make the connection between what they are providing and the goals of the affluent—contributes to their financial success.

Communicating value can take a number of forms. One of the approaches that has been shown both empirically and in the field to be most effective is using high-net-worth psychology.

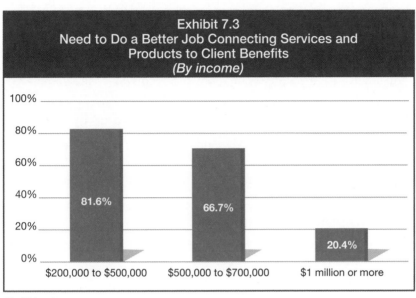

Exhibit 7.3
Need to Do a Better Job Connecting Services and
Products to Client Benefits
(By income)

N = 394 partners.
Source: AES Nation.

High-net-worth psychology

High-net-worth psychology can enable you to more powerfully connect with your wealthy clients and prospective clients. The power of high-net-worth psychology is that it facilitates your ability to frame your services and products so you show your wealthy clients that you fully understand their needs, wants, and goals and that your services and products deliver intended results.

High-net-worth psychology can be exceedingly effective in creating the framework for understanding the specific goals, needs, wants and agendas of wealthy individuals. Moreover, high-net-worth psychology is extraordinarily applicable to creating the messaging that drives wealthy clients and prospective clients to act on your advice.

The high-net-worth psychology framework was developed decades ago using well-established research protocols for creating psychographic segments—or personalities—using surveys of thousands of affluent individuals and multidimensional statistical tools. Since the framework's conception, many elite professionals serving the wealthy, among them accountants, private client lawyers, financial advisors in multifamily offices, and wealth managers, have embraced high-net-worth psychology.

High-net-worth psychology has been one of the most rigorously tested frameworks in the private wealth industry. Its widespread use is a testament to its reliability and effectiveness. The following is an overview of the nine high-net-worth personalities and some of their key attributes.

Family Stewards

- Want to use their wealth to take care of their families

- Want to relieve their family members of financial worries

- Want to fulfill their familial obligations

Independents

- See attention to financial and legal issues as a necessary evil

- Want personal freedom

- Want to have a safety net if they want to or need to bail out

Phobics

- Hate being involved in complex decisions

- Not at all knowledgeable about financial or legal strategies

- Dislike discussing technical issues

Anonymous

- Confidentiality concerning legal matters is key

- Secretive about their financial and legal arrangements

- Extreme privacy is essential for personal comfort

Moguls

- Worldly success is a way of keeping score and winning

- Desire considerable power and control over their affairs

- Seek personal influence

VIPs

- Success is a way to achieve high status

- Want to be well-known and respected

- Seek prestige

Accumulators

- Their top goal is asset accumulation

- Want to retain wealth and add to it

- Their sole objective is to make money

Gamblers

- Treat dealing with financial and legal matters somewhat as a hobby

- Derive pleasure from complexity and machinations

- Relish the problem-solving process

Innovators

- Perceive financial and legal matters to be an intellectual challenge

- Want to be on the cutting edge of tax planning

- Want to employ state-of-the-art wealth management strategies and products

The *Family Steward* is the most prevalent high-net-worth personality. Family Stewards are motivated by the need to protect their families over the long term. They fear for the safety of their families and are highly motivated to organize defenses against external threats. This motivation makes them excellent candidates for a variety of services and products. When working with Family Stewards, you should demonstrably connect your recommendations to the need to create long-term protection for the wealthy individual and his or her family.

Independents are individuals whose primary objective for accumulating wealth is achieving financial independence and the accompanying security. Some want to retire from their financial obligations to play golf or go sailing, while others will continue to work but value the security of knowing they could leave at any time. You should show Independents how a given product or service will foster their goal of personal freedom, while communicating your appreciation of their intentions and values.

The *Phobic* is typically a wealthy individual who dislikes thinking about money and the concerns that money brings. Phobics also have significant control issues because they do not believe they are capable of effectively managing their own financial affairs. Further, they do not think they are especially capable of effectively managing advisors such as their accountants. When working with a Phobic, it is important to provide simple, clear explanations and to effectively partner with the other trusted advisors to whom the Phobic turns for assistance.

Anonymous affluent clients and prospective clients are typified by their deep-seated—and sometimes irrational—need for privacy and confidentiality in all their financial affairs. To work effectively with an Anonymous client, you should demonstrate that you assiduously protect confidentiality, and you should regularly communicate your respect for the need for privacy.

Moguls are motivated to accumulate more and more wealth to achieve personal power (and, by extension, influence and control). They want to leverage the power conferred by wealth. You should acknowledge the Mogul's need for control and power and take care to show how any recommended services and products will maintain or increase the Mogul's control.

VIPs are motivated to accumulate assets and use their wealth to achieve greater status and prestige. VIPs want to be thought well of, especially by other VIPs. As a result, they are more likely than any other high-net-worth personality to seek the external symbols of wealth. They see such symbols as badges of their exalted status. You should show you understand this need for status and respect and should also relate their situation to similar cases among the "rich and famous" wherever possible.

Accumulators seek to acquire wealth out of an overriding concern for personal financial well-being. Unlike other high-net-worth personalities, Accumulators do not seek to achieve family security or emblems of wealth or power. Instead, their focus is on the continual accumulation and protection of assets as a bulwark against an uncertain future. You should acknowledge these individuals' need for wealth and relate your recommendations to their need for capital accumulation and protection.

Gamblers believe that their skills and competence will protect them from all significant threats. They view financial affairs as a personal challenge, but one that they are very capable of handling. You can work with this high-net-worth personality effectively if you share nuances of services and products. You should also talk with Gamblers about the risks and rewards of alternative financial solutions.

Innovators believe their analytical capabilities will sustain and protect them from external threats. Because of their lifelong reliance on their analytic capabilities, they are highly self-reliant and do not completely delegate any portion of life tasks having to do with analysis. You should share the details of technical aspects of the services and products you recommend and involve them in the heady technical details.

Communicating about services and products using high-net-worth psychology

By capitalizing on an understanding that wealthy individuals are very different in their attitudes toward their wealth and the challenges that having significant wealth brings, you are in a much better position to effectively communicate with them.

In discussing a tax plan with a Family Steward, for example, you can show how the elements of the proposed strategies relate to his or her goal of using assets to safeguard the family. Detailed technical discussions may be fine, as long as they always link back to the client's overriding objective of making sure his or her family is well taken care of.

Communicating a tax plan to a Phobic will be very different. Phobics do not want detailed information. They need to make these difficult decisions without personally going into the details. The best way to help this kind of wealthy client is to work closely with his or her other advisors, because a Phobic is reassured when his or her accountant, attorney and wealth manager all agree on a course of action.

Exhibit 7.4 illustrates how high-net-worth personalities differ in their communication needs. By skillfully using the high-net-worth psychology framework, you can be surer of several outcomes. You can be increasingly assured that your wealthy clients feel that you fully understand their goals, needs and preferences and that they are motivated to take action.

To garner the best results, you need to connect with wealthy clients and prospective clients about what is truly important to them. High-net-worth psychology enables you to much better achieve this objective. Family Stewards, for instance, are not interested in offshore trusts; they are interested in their families. Phobics are not concerned with the mechanics of tax-wise charitable giving. Instead, they want someone else to take care of the matter for them.

It's worthwhile to keep in mind that by employing high-net-worth psychology, you are not changing the nature or character of your services and products. All you are doing is explaining your expertise in ways that meaningfully resonate with wealthy clients and prospective clients.

Exhibit 7.4 High-Net-Worth Personalities and Accountant Communications	
High-net-worth personality	**Needs from accountants**
Family Stewards	• Communicate how services and products will protect family interests. • Stress involvement of key family members.
Independents	• Show how services and products will foster their goal of personal freedom. • Communicate an appreciation of the high-net-worth client's values.
Phobics	• Structure simple and clear explanations of proposed services and products. • Work effectively with other trusted advisors.
Anonymous	• Demonstrate that confidentiality is assiduously protected. • Communicate respect for their privacy needs.
Moguls	• Acknowledge their need for control and power. • Show how services and products will maintain or increase their ability to influence others.
VIPs	• Show an understanding of their need for status and respect. • Relate their situation to cases among the "rich and famous."
Accumulators	• Acknowledge their need for wealth accumulation. • Relate services and products to their need to amass and protect capital.
Gamblers	• Share the nuances of services and products. • Talk with them about the risks and rewards of possible financial solutions.
Innovators	• Share details of the technical aspects of the recommended services and products. • Focus on state-of-the-art financial solutions.

Example: Communicating the value of a charitable trust

There are certain services and products widely employed by the Super Rich, family offices and ultra-wealthy business owners that are increasingly applicable to a much wider affluent audience. A charitable trust is but one example of such a service or product.

As we've seen, being able to address a particular product (as a product-neutral accountant) or to deliver the product (as a product-inclusive accountant) is becoming more and more important to serving affluent clients effectively and to differentiating your high-net-worth accounting practice from the wide array of professionals courting and serving the wealthy.

But expertise—while essential—is insufficient to garner a $1 million or more annual income. You must be able to easily communicate the value of any proposed service or product to wealthy clients and prospective clients in a way that inspires them to action.

The following are very simplified examples intended to demonstrate how high-net-worth psychology can be used to connect a proposed charitable trust with what matters most to each of the high-net-worth personalities. (In these examples, we assume, of course, that the client is charitably minded.)

Family Stewards

"Not only does the charitable trust help support a cause that's important to you, but setting it up also shows your kids the importance of giving back."

Independents

"By creating an income stream through this charitable trust, you're going to much sooner be able to decide if it's time to chuck the job and retire in the style you want."

Phobics

"Your attorney and I have come up with an IRS-approved way for you to pay less taxes and help the causes you care about. Together, we'll take care of all the details for you."

Anonymous

"What's very appealing about what we're doing is that we're able to accomplish your charitable goals yet do so while keeping all information concerning your assets highly confidential."

Moguls

"By funding this charitable trust for your alma mater, you'll be able to help set the direction for the future of the college. They may even ask you to join the board of trustees."

VIPs

"More and more, the wealthiest and smartest investors in the world are reducing their estate taxes and making a recognizable difference in the world by doing what you're going to be doing."

Accumulators

"This will enable you to turn your non-income-producing property—which isn't giving you anything right now—into an income stream while you support the causes that matter to you. This will let you build up your investment portfolio a lot faster."

Gamblers

"This is a great way of completely legally beating the house. There are a lot of technical aspects, which we'll discuss, but there's no question this approach will let you benefit from the tax laws, help the charities you care about and come out way ahead of the IRS."

Innovators

"This type of charitable trust is state-of-the-art tax planning. This isn't a cookie-cutter solution, so executing it properly and getting all the advantages requires a high degree of technical expertise."

Our intent with these examples is to provide you with some perspective. Your ability to skillfully integrate high-net-worth psychology in all your interactions with your wealthy clients and prospective clients will enable you to build stronger and more meaningful relationships with them and make it immensely easier for you to get their buy-in.

Food for thought

Accountants often fail to connect their services and products with what really matters to the wealthy. For the affluent, it is almost always about the outcomes. It is regularly about how they benefit and prosper and not about the particularities of the products and services. It is very informative that most accountants recognize they are not doing as good a job as they possibly could to communicate value.

High-net-worth psychology is a verified methodology that can empower you to ensure that your recommendations and solutions strongly resonate with the wealthy. As we noted, high-net-worth psychology is not about doing what you do technically any differently. Instead, it is a way for you to better relate to the wealthy—resulting in your advice being more readily accepted and your client relationships deepening.

CHAPTER 8

Maximize Wealthy Client Relationships

Finding wealthy prospective clients and converting them into clients is most often a considerable task. Even when you create strategic partnerships with other professionals—something we will discuss in the next chapter—a lot of time and energy go into maintaining and enhancing those relationships. And even then, wealthy individuals still need to be motivated to engage you.

It therefore only makes good business sense—once you have new wealthy clients—to maximize the services and products you provide them. This is not only very beneficial to your wealthy clients; it helps you on the path to establishing a high-net-worth accounting practice that can earn you at least $1 million a year.

In many ways, maximizing wealthy client relationships is like picking low-hanging fruit. Your wealthy clients are accessible, and provided you deliver outstanding value, more than likely to use the additional services and products you recommend.

Low-hanging fruit

The term "low-hanging fruit" refers to easily obtainable gains. It is a metaphor for pursuing the simplest and easiest path to results first. Where is fruit hanging lowest? The answer lies in your own affluent clientele.

More than three-quarters of the accountants surveyed said there are substantial additional services and products they could be providing to their wealthy clients, but that they are not doing so. (See Exhibit 8.1.) In our experience, a large percentage of accountants are reticent about actively pursuing additional business unless the affluent client has clearly expressed a need for additional services or products.

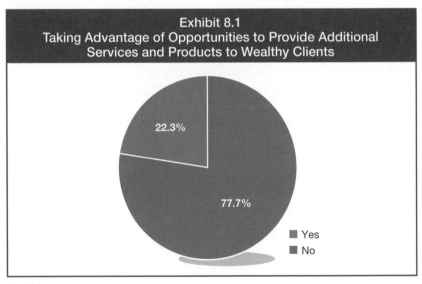

Exhibit 8.1
Taking Advantage of Opportunities to Provide Additional Services and Products to Wealthy Clients

22.3%

77.7%

■ Yes
■ No

N = 394 partners.
Source: AES Nation.

Proportionately more product-neutral than product-inclusive accountants say they are failing to leverage opportunities. At the same time, it is the elite accountants who are doing a superior job for their wealthy clients, as most are providing them—directly or by referral—multiple services and products. (See Exhibits 8.2 and 8.3.)

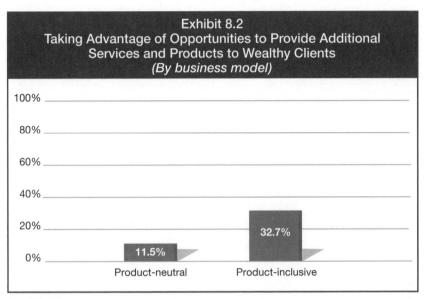

Exhibit 8.2
Taking Advantage of Opportunities to Provide Additional Services and Products to Wealthy Clients
(By business model)

N = 394 partners.
Source: AES Nation.

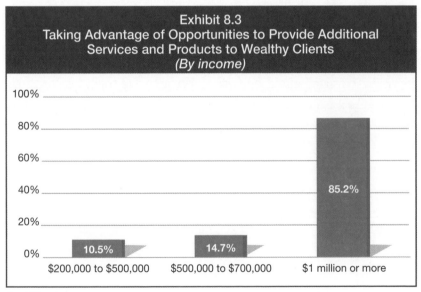

Exhibit 8.3
Taking Advantage of Opportunities to Provide Additional Services and Products to Wealthy Clients
(By income)

N = 394 partners.
Source: AES Nation.

The key to plucking the low-hanging fruit is having a broad and deep understanding of your wealthy clients. The extended capabilities of your accounting firm are a major factor that will have a great impact on how well you can capitalize on these opportunities. However, even if your accounting firm can benefit from these circumstances, you must be systematic and proactive to take full advantage.

The Total Client Model

To build and maintain a high-net-worth accounting practice that provides you with a yearly income of $1 million or more, you must be able to address the immediate concerns and issues facing your wealthy clients while maintaining the holistic perspective that allows for long-term planning and achievement of goals. It is often essential for you and your staff to understand the priorities and preferences of your wealthy clients on a real-time basis.

One way to acquire this level of understanding is to use profiling processes to develop a comprehensive assessment of a wealthy individual that can be easily translated into actionable and customized solutions. The Total Client Model is one such profiling process. As client assets increase in size and complexity, it is even more important that you utilize a profiling process or methodology on a regular basis to stay abreast of milestones, external factors and other material changes that can impact your wealthy clients.

For all intents and purposes, it is not possible for you to learn too much about your wealthy clients. The more you know about them, the better you can serve them. Over decades, we have tapped the experience and know-how of elite professionals who have large numbers of extremely satisfied wealthy clients, so we could develop a framework for information-gathering that any professional can use to assess client needs, wants, preferences and—very importantly—new business opportunities.

The framework we devised is called the Total Client Model. Exhibit 8.4 provides a visual overview of its seven categories.

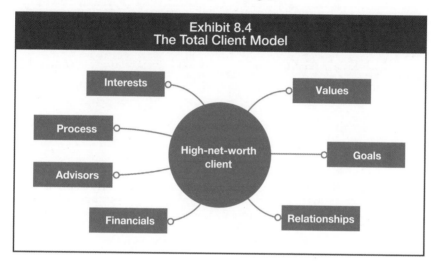

The following are sample questions for each category:

Values

- What social issues are very important to the client?

- What is the client's religious orientation? How devout is he or she?

- What specific values does the client feel are important to communicate to heirs?

Goals

- What are the client's personal and professional goals?

- What does the client want to do, or feel obligated to do, for his or her children, other family members, friends, society, and the world at large?

- What are the client's aspirations for his or her loved ones?

Relationships

- Which family relationships (spouse, children, siblings, parents, etc.) are most important in the client's personal and professional lives?

- Who are the client's business associates? How important are they to the client?

- What are the client's particularly strong business relationships?

Financials

- How are the client's assets structured?

- How is the client currently managing his or her financial assets?

- How does the client make money today? How is that likely to change in the next three years?

Advisors

- Who are the client's other advisors? What role does each advisor play?

- How frequently has the client switched advisors recently?

- Which advisors are especially close to the client?

Process

- Who else should be in the room when services and products are presented to the client?

- What security measures are being used to protect the client's personal and financial information?

- How detailed should the explanation of legal strategies be when presented to the client?

Interests

- What are the client's favorite activities, TV programs, movies and sports teams?

- What charities are important to the client?

- Are health and fitness important to the client? If so, what is his or her regimen?

The Total Client Model is illustrated as sets of questions. However, we do not advise that you ask all these questions directly. The more effective approach is to make open-ended queries during a careful and systematic discovery process. As you collect information, you can fill in the answers to the extensive sets of questions in each category.

The Total Client Model is being used successfully by all manner of professionals working with the wealthy. We have extensively coached accountants, private client lawyers, wealth managers, financial advisors, private bankers, consultants and life insurance agents in how to use it.

The framework enables all of these professionals to obtain a deep understanding of their wealthy clients. By knowing the possibilities presented by different fact patterns, you are likely to uncover more opportunities to create high levels of client satisfaction and generate more business.

Common mistakes to avoid when using the Total Client Model

With appropriate commitment and practice, most any accountant can become proficient at using the Total Client Model. To help abbreviate that process, we have identified the most common oversights of inexperienced practitioners:

- **Focusing intensely on their specialties.** Accountants are well-served by thinking beyond their own expertise. The better you are able to recognize opportunities that cannot be solved exclusively by your services and products, the better it is for you and for your affluent clients. Moreover, it can be extremely useful to be able to identify issues, concerns and possible solutions that extend beyond the financial and legal environments. One example is the applicability of concierge health care to wealthy clients facing complex or ongoing health challenges.

- **Taking too much for granted.** Many accountants make all sorts of assumptions about their wealthy clients. Over time, it is usually a good idea to verify these assumptions, as some of them may be inaccurate. By correcting the impreciseness, you will likely regularly open the door to new revenue possibilities.

- **Not regularly refining and updating wealthy clients' profiles.** People's lives are in a perpetual state of flux. While many—perhaps all—accountants know this to be true, they usually fail to capitalize on it. It is generally a good idea to review the profiles of wealthy clients over time to spot changes and the opportunities they provide.

Discerning possibilities

Using the Total Client Model, you will be able to collect and organize a considerable amount of pertinent and applicable data. By using this fact-coordinating tool, you will likely find certain gaps in your knowledge about some of your wealthy clients. Moreover, as you close these gaps, new business opportunities will regularly present themselves.

The key to moving from "knowing" to "doing" is your ability and, when appropriate, your team's ability to discern fact patterns and recognize possible solutions.

A good place to start is with the affluent client's goals and critical concerns. They are the drivers determining what your wealthy client will consider and will not want to be bothered with. Then the financials come into play. You want to understand the mix and arrangement of assets and liabilities so you can provide financial solutions and alternatives. Both business and personal relationships are instrumental in setting parameters. In addition, the interests of your wealthy clients—primarily their charitable interests—will usually prove important.

Over our decades of working with professionals to construct detailed understandings of their affluent clients using the Total Client Model, we have found that many opportunities repeat themselves. To help you with some of the common and recurring opportunities, we have identified a number of high-probability situations. We have found that as professionals become more and more practiced with the Total Client Model, they become very adept at spotting the opportunities.

115

For each of the following high-probability opportunities, we first highlight what to watch for. Then we point out the likely problems and some potential solutions. In each of these examples, we have also included a talking point that can be used to prompt clients to act or consider acting.

What to watch for: highly concentrated stock positions

- Problem: lack of diversification

- Potential solutions:

  - Create a well-diversified investment portfolio.

  - Sell positions using charitable trusts.

  - Employ various hedging strategies.

- Talking point: "Are you comfortable with having such a large percentage of your wealth in a single stock?"

What to watch for: affluent clients with special needs children

- Problem: ensuring the care and treatment of their children, no matter what

- Potential solutions:

  - Develop cost projections for the care of the child.

  - Establish a special needs trust.

  - Structure or oversee the structuring of an investment portfolio to address the child's income requirements.

- Talking point: "Have you taken all the steps possible to make sure Robert is financially secure?"

What to watch for: an estate plan that is five or more years old

- Problems:

    - An estate plan that does not provide the resolution the affluent client wants

    - A life insurance policy that is just as old as the estate plan

- Potential solutions:

    - Review the current estate plan and make adjustments if there are gaps.

    - Do a 1035 exchange of the life insurance or select a new policy.

- Talking point: "If you could have the exact same life insurance coverage for less cost, would you be interested?"

What to watch for: teenage children driving vehicles titled in their parents' names or owned by their parents' company

- Problem: If the child is in a car accident where someone is injured or killed, the parents may be liable.

- Potential solutions:

    - Select trusts or corporate structures to shield the assets of the parents.

    - Purchase maximum liability insurance.

- Talking point: "If your son hits a bus full of preschool children and someone on the bus is badly hurt or killed, the lawsuit will cut right through your umbrella policy and everything you own may be lost."

What to watch for: affluent clients with second or third marriages, or blended families

- Problem: the desire for estate equalization and related concerns among the respective families and children

- Potential solutions:

    - Ensure that the estate plan is current.

    - Have money in individual accounts or in trusts for family members.

    - Use life insurance, if necessary, for estate equalization.

- Talking point: "Are you interested in all the children inheriting equally?"

What to watch for: valuable collections, such as artwork and jewelry

- Problems:

    - The collection is not secure.

    - The insurance may not be adequate to replace lost pieces of the collection.

- Potential solutions:

    - Take all reasonable steps to ensure the protection of the collection.

    - Obtain an up-to-date appraisal of the collection and make sure it is properly insured.

- Talking point: "When was the last time you took a good look at the value of your collection?"

What to watch for: a business owner with equity partners

- Problem: Ownership of the business goes to someone the remaining partners do not want to work with, such as the deceased's spouse.

- Potential solution: Have an up-to-date buy/sell agreement funded by the appropriate investments or life insurance.

- Talking point: "Do you want to be in business with your partner's spouse?"

What to watch for: assets such as intellectual property that have income streams that continue after death

- Problem: Creates a taxable event for heirs because the total value of the asset may be subject to any estate taxes that may be owed

- Potential solutions:

  - Structure the estate so that the value of the income stream is preserved for the client's loved ones.

  - Take out life insurance to pay any estate taxes that may be owed.

- Talking point: "Do you care if the government, instead of your family, gets 50 percent or more of the value of your patent when you die?"

What to watch for: potential future divorce

- Problem: a case of fraudulent conveyance if the assets are moved at the wrong time

- Potential solutions:

    - Redo the affluent client's estate plan while the couple is still together.

    - Use trusts to hold assets pre-divorce.

    - Use asset protection strategies in advance of the divorce.

- Talking point: "Are you interested in some ideas to keep your money out of the hands of that gold digger?"

What to watch for: affluent clients who plan to sell their companies in the future

- Problem: The value of the company is expected to increase, resulting in the need to pay more in estate taxes.

- Potential solutions:

    - Ensure the financial statements effectively convey the value of the business.

    - "Freeze" the value of the business using various trusts or partnerships.

- Talking point: "Are you interested in potentially saving more than $X million in future estate taxes?"

While these are fairly common situations, how each one needs to be managed can be very different. Moreover, the potential solutions we have provided are on the very basic side of things. There are many ways—often more sophisticated ones—of accomplishing these results.

While these types of business opportunities proliferate, the real world is usually a lot messier. It is often a combination of data points—multifaceted fact patterns—that really gives rise to business opportunities. By skillfully working with your team, you will be able to address these more-complex scenarios. (See *Chapter 5: Build and Manage Your Expert Team.*)

Client-focused business development plans

Many accountants write business development plans. While these plans certainly have a role in helping set the direction and certain activities of a high-net-worth accounting practice, they can be limited in their ability to deliver substantial results. We see numerous weaknesses in many business development plans, from not being tied to specific anticipated outcomes to being put on the shelf until they are pulled out by the accountant a year or so later and rewritten.

Instead of creating an overarching business development plan, construct client-focused business development plans that are informed by the insights you gathered using the Total Client Model. Very simply, client-focused business development plans specify the business opportunities you recognized and how you are going to convert these possibilities into viable deliverables for your wealthy clients.

For each wealthy client you have evaluated using the Total Client Model, we recommend that you write a detailed plan for executing on the new business opportunities you identified. Include the potential referrals to new wealthy clients. This plan is very likely the greatest value you can deliver to your wealthy clients, and it is something that can also provide great value to your practice.

We have found that once astute accountants become comfortable in creating basic client-focused business development plans, they can "level up." This entails projecting revenue numbers for possible new business, in addition to the monies they could reasonably earn from sourcing new wealthy clients through client referrals. While these numbers tend to be somewhat off-target, they are very often directionally accurate. This permits you to triage opportunities more effectively.

It is important to remember that client-focused business development plans are always evolving. As you become more and more familiar and proficient with the process, you will probably uncover new and creative ways to build your high-net-worth accounting practice. In addition, as your wealthy clients' situations change or external forces impact their lives, you will regularly be better-prepared to expeditiously take action that will result in delivering tremendous value to them and more revenue for your practice.

Food for thought

Most accountants recognize they can do more than they are currently doing for their affluent clients. In contrast, elite accountants tend to be very good at identifying additional opportunities to deliver value to their wealthy clients and at delivering that value. Not only is this characteristic of being truly client-centered, but it is also an effective way to create personal wealth. It's a win-win for everyone.

By mastering the Total Client Model, you will likely become significantly more client-centered. With your team (see *Chapter 5: Build and Manage Your Expert Team*), you will be able to identify and deliver additional services and products that will better the lives of your wealthy clients.

CHAPTER 9

Generate Referrals from Other Professionals

There are many ways to build a top-of-the-line accounting practice for the wealthy. Acquisitions, for example, is one approach. Still, for the vast majority of accountants, the cornerstone for creating a high-net-worth accounting practice that earns you $1 million or more annually is being able to source new wealthy clients. However, as we saw in *Chapter 1: Accountants Under Pressure*, nearly nine out of ten accountants surveyed said it is quite difficult to source new wealthy clients.

There are many ways to potentially source high-net-worth clients. Some of the common approaches include:

- Generating client referrals

- Generating referrals from other professionals

- Presenting at seminars, workshops and other events

- Conducting social media outreach

- Cold-calling

Some approaches are indisputably more effective than others. Without question, one of the most powerful ways to build a highly successful high-net-worth accounting practice is to generate referrals from other professionals.

Garnering new wealthy clients from other professionals

We have consistently and empirically found that most professionals get their best wealthy clients from other professionals. And this is indeed the case for the great majority of surveyed accountants, as Exhibit 9.1 shows.

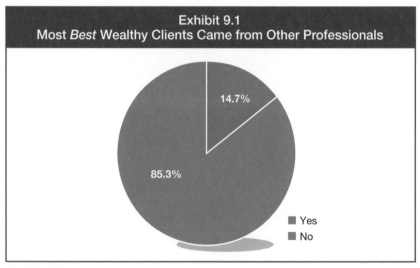

N = 394 partners.
Source: AES Nation.

This remains the case irrespective of business model. And as you move up the income scale, you are probably going to find that referrals from other professionals are the optimal—if not the only—way to source ultra-wealthy clients. (See Exhibits 9.2 and 9.3.)

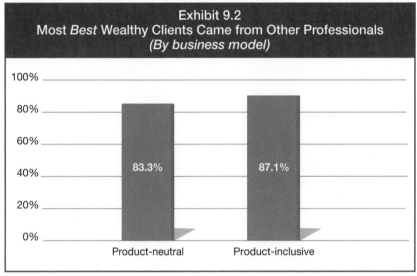

Exhibit 9.2
Most *Best* Wealthy Clients Came from Other Professionals
(By business model)

N = 394 partners.
Source: AES Nation.

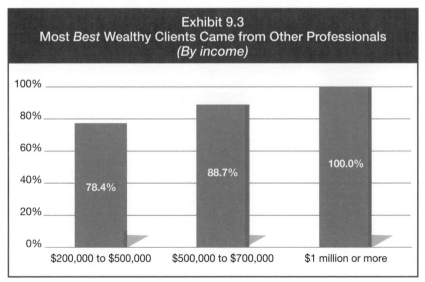

Exhibit 9.3
Most *Best* Wealthy Clients Came from Other Professionals
(By income)

N = 394 partners.
Source: AES Nation.

To be clear: Whatever is working for you now in garnering new wealthy clients is something you should certainly continue. Still, in order to build an extremely successful high-net-worth accounting practice, you are probably going to have to work with wealthier clients, and being able to consistently source them from other professionals is the best new-client business development approach.

As seen in Exhibit 9.4, we also found that nine out of ten accountants believe they could do a much better job of sourcing new wealthy clients from other professionals.

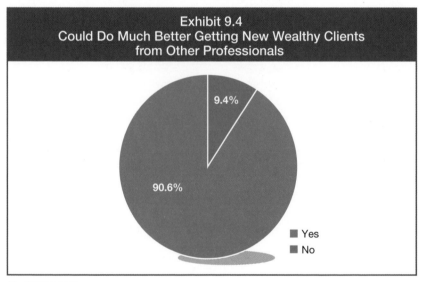

Exhibit 9.4
Could Do Much Better Getting New Wealthy Clients from Other Professionals

9.4%

90.6%

■ Yes
■ No

N = 394 partners.
Source: AES Nation.

There is no meaningful difference between product-neutral and product-inclusive accountants when it comes to believing they could do much better at getting new wealthy clients, although proportionately slightly fewer elite accountants take this view. (See Exhibits 9.5 and 9.6.)

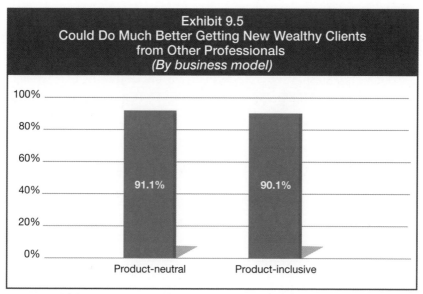

Exhibit 9.5
Could Do Much Better Getting New Wealthy Clients
from Other Professionals
(By business model)

N = 394 partners.
Source: AES Nation.

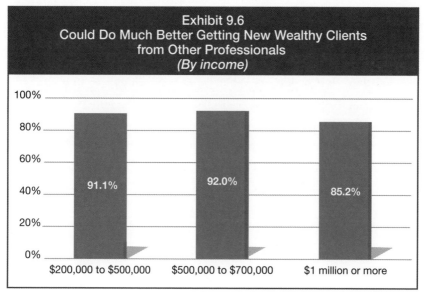

Exhibit 9.6
Could Do Much Better Getting New Wealthy Clients
from Other Professionals
(By income)

N = 394 partners.
Source: AES Nation.

There is little doubt that the great majority of accountants recognize the power of sourcing new wealthy clients from other professionals. They also recognize that they can do a better job of making this happen. Accountants who smartly and systematically build strategic partnerships are better able to build exceptional practices that can earn them $1 million or more per year.

The power of referrals from other professionals

There are two interrelated reasons that referrals from other professionals are so very effective in enabling you to build an exceptional high-net-worth accounting practice: access and influential introductions. Other professionals working with the wealthy, such as private client lawyers and bankers, spend their time with their affluent clients addressing matters that overlap with your services and products.

Moreover, experts in related fields can make influential introductions because these professionals:

- **Validate your expertise.** When other professionals recommend you and say that you are one of the very best professionals for the job, your ability to get the business increases exponentially. It is optimal when the other professional can provide a rationale and materials that support your capabilities and talents, such as evidence that you are a thought leader. (See *Chapter 6: Become a Thought Leader.*)

- **Emphasize a personal fit.** When other professionals tell their wealthy clients that they will have good rapport with you, your ability to close business dramatically increases. The other professionals are emphasizing not only that you can do a great job, but that you're also a good person to do business with and that the wealthy individual or family will like you.

- **Provide impetus to action.** When other professionals say to their wealthy clients, "You need this accountant's expertise and you need it now," the affluent clients are much more inclined not only to engage you, but to do so expeditiously.

In these situations, the hard-earned, high-quality business and personal relationships other professionals share with their wealthy clients are, to varying degrees, transferred to you. To make this happen on a fairly consistent basis, you must create strategic partnerships.

The advantage of strategic partnerships

Strategic partnerships are a special type of relationship between professionals. They differ dramatically from what are commonly called strategic relationships. Exhibit 9.7 compares the two.

Exhibit 9.7 Strategic Relationships Compared with Strategic Partnerships	
Strategic relationships	**Strategic partnerships**
A wealthy client is periodically pointed in your direction.	The other professional introduces you to his or her wealthy clients on a regular basis and actively lobbies on your behalf.
You are one of a number of accounting professionals being considered.	You are the only or primary accounting authority for the other professional's wealthy clients.
Most opportunities are driven by the wealthy clients and not by the other professional.	The other professional is vigorously looking to make strong introductions of his or her wealthy clients to you.

Professionals you have a strategic relationship with will possibly refer a new wealthy client to you once in a while. When they do make these referrals, you should not be surprised if you are one of several accountants the other professional names for their wealthy client to consider. Most telling in these situations is that it is the wealthy clients who usually prompt the other professional to make a referral.

In contrast, strategic partnerships support you directly. These other professionals are exceedingly proactive in finding wealthy clients for you. When they share their wealthy clients with you, they do not even consider anyone else.

The street-smart networking process

To source the best high-net-worth clients, you would be well-advised to create strategic partnerships with other professionals who have wealthy clients. By evaluating the way elite professionals with differing expertise build strategic partnerships, we systematized the process. We call it street-smart networking.

Street smarts largely define many of the most financially accomplished professionals working with the wealthy. Street-smart networking is the methodology tremendously successful professionals use to connect with other professionals, resulting in a steady stream of new high-net-worth clients. The following actions are instrumental to the approach.

- **Set high but grounded aspirations.** Street-smart networking starts with your aspirations. Having notable and often lofty goals tends to foster a virtuous cycle of motivation and actions. It also sets the baseline for measuring success and enables refinement.

- **Advance the agenda.** With your goals in place, preparation is essential. You need to put together a plan. Very successful professionals prove to be very good at determining what it is going to take to enable them to achieve their high but grounded aspirations. They often develop an understanding by being astute, lifelong learners, coupled with being constructively self-critical.

- **Conduct assessments.** The ability to ably evaluate other professionals is regularly at the very core of extraordinary networking success. This commonly involves making extreme efforts to develop a broad and deep understanding of the other professionals you are connecting with (see our discussion of assessing other professionals below).

- **Ensure alignment.** You must align the other professional's interests with your own. This is solidly predicated on street smarts. Aligned interests are usually based on a deep understanding of the other professional's critical concerns first and his or her expressed intent second.

- **Measure achievements.** To achieve optimal results, you must make sure everything is on track. This entails regularly comparing your results with your aspirations. When there's a disconnect, you are then able to make the requisite adjustments.

Street-smart networking is a highly systematic and thoughtful framework for identifying and working with other professionals to achieve significant results. It is a mindful and exacting set of means that fosters intense success and regularly and constructively opens up considerable new business possibilities.

The Assessment Instrument

In many respects, the heart of street-smart networking is the Assessment Instrument, which is similar to the Total Client Model we discussed in the previous chapter. (See Exhibit 9.8.)

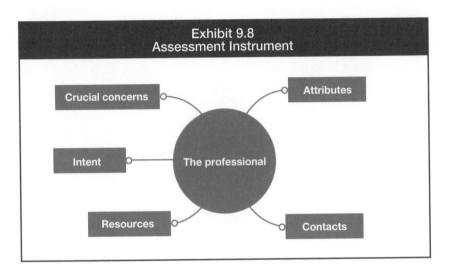

There are many ways of cataloging the information you want from other professionals, but we'll consider—in broad strokes, with a few examples—the components of the Assessment Instrument.

Attributes

Attributes are the central and often defining characteristics of the person. We usually look to address the following attributes:

- Demographics:

  - Personal factors

  - Years in business

  - Wealth

- Professional situation:

  - Technical expertise and specific competencies

- Strengths and weaknesses

- A comprehensive understanding of their business model

To ensure a solid and ongoing alignment of interests, you must understand the other professional's situation. You will also need to be keenly aware of their goals (which we will address below), as well as how the professional achieves these goals, based on their particular business model.

Contacts

Contacts are the people the other professional knows and can access. There are many components to this category, and you need to ascertain all these facets. These are the most pressing and informative components:

- Nature of contacts:

  - The affluent with whom they do business

  - The types of affluent clients they have

  - Other relevant relationships they have

- Source of contacts:

  - Through business connections

  - Through family connections

  - Through social connections

- Strength of contacts:

  - Support they have provided, with examples

- Support they have obtained, with examples

- Obligations they owe and are owed

- Connector capabilities:

  - Extended contacts—second and third spheres beyond direct contacts

  - The quality of these extended relationships

  - Obligations they owe and are owed beyond direct contacts

The single degree of separation of affluent clients' contacts is usually the most important one for building your wealthy clientele. You need to determine the number of potential wealthy clients as well as the quality of their relationships.

Resources

Resources are the "assets" and means at the other professional's disposal. This goes beyond the people they know and can influence. It's important to be able to get your mind around these other possibilities. This is what you want to know:

- Access to resources:

  - Types of resources that are available to the professional

  - Form of control with respect to these resources (this is most commonly either direct or indirect)

  - Degree of applicability and leveragability and how these resources can prove beneficial

It is not only whom the other professional knows, but also his or her ability to deliver other resources that can prove quite useful in enabling you to acquire new affluent clients. The other professional's firm's marketing capabilities, for example, can be very helpful to all parties in accessing new wealthy clients.

Intent

Intent refers to the other professional's preferences, needs and wants as they translate into interim objectives, which feed into larger goals. These various goals and objectives are evidenced in their needs and wants, so they must be taken into account. There are three categories of goals:

*   Financial goals:

    *   The other professional's financial end goal

    *   Financial goals for various business initiatives

    *   The gaps between current status and goals

*   Strategic business goals:

    *   Business stature and positioning, with examples

    *   Explicit planned and tactical objectives, including methodologies and operational considerations

    *   The principal obstacles to achieving expressed and unexpressed strategic business goals

- Personal goals:

  - Nonfinancial goals for their family and themselves

  - Their philanthropic aims and particular charitable activities

  - The expressed and unexpressed impediments to reaching these goals

When you are choosing other professionals you want to convert into strategic partners, we habitually recommend that they have high financial end goals. It is quite helpful if they are "hungry" and very keen on becoming more successful in their careers.

Crucial concerns

Crucial concerns are the dominant and persuasive issues and interests the other professional is presently dealing with. Everyone is a "naked emperor." Simply put, you need to know the following:

- Issues and matters that are top-of-mind to the professional:

  - Concerns that are dramatically impacting decision-making

  - Concerns that affect their ability to focus, respond and follow through

  - Concerns that result in dysfunctional behavior, with examples

While all the categories are important and useful to understanding whether another professional can be a strategic partner, the critical concerns category is the most telling.

Food for thought

Elite accountants and other extremely successful professionals tend be very capable at establishing and maintaining strategic partnerships. While there are many ways to source new wealthy clients, garnering them from other professionals proves to be the most viable way to source the wealthy—especially the ultra-wealthy and Super Rich.

A proven methodology for creating strategic partnerships is street-smart networking. It's a highly systematic process for creating a steady stream of new wealthy clients. Core to street-smart networking is the Assessment Instrument.

We have been teaching and facilitating the street-smart networking process for decades. We have found that most any motivated professional can become quite adept with the methodology, resulting in establishing and enhancing powerful strategic partnerships.

CONCLUSION

Building an Exceptional High-Net-Worth Practice

It is an undeniable fact that the accounting industry is being transformed. A plethora of factors are impacting the industry, with many of them potentially detrimental to the success of accountants. The result of these changes is that a considerable number of accountants are more likely to see their incomes and wealth diminish rather than rise. This is the stark reality in spite of the fact that most accountants say they really want to be wealthier than they are today.

Trends such as greater competition from non-accountants, the commoditization of expertise and fee pressure are only going to intensify. All these factors combine to very plausibly drive down the earning power, incomes and wealth of accountants.

All that said, outstanding opportunities remain for accountants to create tremendous value for themselves and their clients. One such possibility is in service to the wealthy. For better or worse, the wealthy are expanding in number and affluence throughout the world. The divide between the affluent and the rest of the world is growing larger, and this trend is likely to continue to intensify. At the same time, the wealthy need and want the expertise high-caliber accountants can provide.

By working with the wealthy, you are putting yourself in the line of money. You can, as many accountants do, concentrate your efforts on particularly high-value affluent clients. For example, for the majority of accountants, the optimal high-net-worth client type will be successful business owners. They have needs and wants that accountants can address, and, because of their business interests, accountants can provide many other types of services and products to them and their companies.

Other high-potential wealthy clients include affluent investors. The "sweet spot" tends to be investors with $500,000 to $10 million in financial assets. For a much smaller number of extraordinarily capable accountants, single-family offices prove to be incredibly worthwhile clients. Single-family offices usually require a panoply of services and products that clever, competent accountants are able to deliver.

If you are reasonably intelligent and highly motivated, it is very possible for you to build a very successful high-net-worth accounting practice that earns you $1 million or more every year. But perseverance is essential, as things rarely go smoothly in building an exceptional high-net-worth accounting practice. Moreover, perseverance has been consistently shown to be an essential quality of people who have become seriously wealthy through their own efforts.

For you to build a high-net-worth accounting practice, a good starting place is deciding on your business model. We discussed two business models: the product-neutral model and the product-inclusive model. Throughout the book, we showed the differences between the two. You can create the quality high-net-worth accounting practice that will enable you to become personally wealthy with either business model. The product-inclusive business model, though more complicated to manage, is also more likely to result—when implemented well—in you earning a great deal of money. The reason: the margin in financial products. Either way, you need to thoughtfully select a business model.

Once you have chosen your business model, you would be well-advised to master the best practices of elite accountants and other professionals who are taking home $1 million or more annually. Although we concentrated on business development best practices in this book, you will need to address a broad array of issues and follow in the footsteps of the most successful accountants working with the wealthy.

When it comes to effective business development, you first have to make certain you have a well-running team supporting you. The wealthy have a multitude of issues and concerns you will probably need and want to address. No one person can handle these matters; they require a team approach. The ability to deliver products and services to the Super Rich can be instrumental to the success of your high-net-worth practice and usually requires tapping the expertise of specialists.

Making sure your team is staffed properly, including with a cadre of specialists, is the responsible and profitable course of action. Furthermore, you have to strongly manage the relationships among team members and make sure everyone is working in the best interests of your wealthy clients.

Most every type of professional has recognized that the wealthy are optimal clients. For the affluent, all these professionals vying for attention create a great deal of noise and confusion. The most effective way for you to cut through the clutter is to become a thought leader. By being a recognized authority for your expertise, you will get appreciably more opportunities to connect with the wealthy.

Being a thought leader is unquestionably very effective in helping you access the wealthy on preferential terms. When you are a thought leader, you are better able to create strategic partnerships as well as garner more referrals from wealthy clients. There are often additional benefits such as shortening the sales cycle and strengthening relationships with existing wealthy clients. Without question, the ability to develop and communicate innovative and meaningful thought leadership content to the wealthy and referral sources can be very useful in building an exceptional high-net-worth accounting practice. For the preponderance of accountants, the most effective and cost-effective way to become a thought leader is to curate content.

For some accountants, one barrier to working with the wealthy and garnering significant revenue is the failure to communicate value. Some accountants commonly get wrapped up in their own expertise and ingenuity, which can befuddle the wealthy or anyone who is not well-versed in the nuances of their services and products. There is a very effective solution to this problem: Frame your deliverables using high-net-worth psychology. Using high-net-worth psychology will enable you to powerfully connect with your wealthy clients and prospective clients. They will increasingly respond positively to your recommendations. Moreover, high-net-worth psychology has been shown to foster client referrals.

Because of the energy usually required to source a new, quality wealthy client, it only makes sense to maximize the relationship. This entails providing additional services and products. To make this happen, you must be proactive in generating new opportunities for your expertise from your current wealthy clients. There are various ways to accomplish this goal, but using the Total Client Model as a basis for creating client-centered business development plans has been consistently proven to be extremely effective.

Always on the best practices list is being able to source new wealthy clients. While there are various ways to accomplish this goal, the most powerful way is usually through referrals from other professionals. This does not negate the importance of client referrals or of reaching out to prospective clients directly, such as through presentations for mastermind and CEO groups. But no matter which type of professional we are dealing with, referrals from other professionals are regularly the optimal way to bring in new wealthy clients.

Methodologies such as street-smart networking are very effective in enabling accountants to build strategic partnerships with other professionals. Strategic partnerships will provide you with a steady stream of new wealthy clients who need your services and products and who are predisposed to work with you.

Another consideration for accountants who want to become seriously wealthy is taking the requisite steps to maximize their personal wealth. This often entails taking chips off the table and benefiting from their own expertise as well as the skills and knowledge of the specialists on their teams.

By making use of Super Rich services and products, for example, accountants can regularly increase and protect their hard-earned wealth. Many of these Super Rich services and products can do the same job for accountants and their firms that they do for the wealthy, thereby helping accountants progress along the path to becoming seriously wealthy.

In conclusion, while it can be challenging for you to become seriously wealthy—to earn $1 million annually—these financial goals can absolutely be achieved. Very telling, when we have coached and consulted with motivated, talented accountants on how to effectively implement the best practices we have discussed, they have been able to considerably increase their revenues, their incomes and their net worth.

The perspectives, processes and strategies we discussed in this book can be transformational for a great many high-net-worth accounting practices. When you enact these effective business development best practices, even at relatively low levels, your earnings can increase arithmetically and sometimes exponentially. Thus, it certainly is possible for you to create an exceptional high-net-worth accounting practice and, when you combine that with astute use of Super Rich services and products, to become seriously wealthy. We wish you the best of success on your journey.